# Basic Concepts in
# Macro Economics

# BASIC CONCEPTS
# IN
# MACRO-ECONOMICS

## Neil Fuller

*B.Sc., M.Sc., M.Inst. P.S.*

**Checkmate/Arnold**

© Checkmate Publications 1984

First published in Great Britain 1984
by Checkmate Publications,
4 Ainsdale Close, Bromborough, Wirral L63 0EU.


and by


Edward Arnold (Publishers) Ltd.,
41 Bedford Square, London WC1B 3DQ

Edward Arnold (Australia) Pty Ltd.,
80 Waverley Road, Caulfield East, Victoria 3145, Australia

Edward Arnold, 3 East Read Street, Baltimore,
Maryland 21202, USA.



Reprinted 1985 and 1987.


ISBN 0 946973 30 X

Text set in 10/12pt Times
by Birkenhead Press Ltd. and Merseyside Graphics Ltd.
Printed & Bound by Richard Clay (The Chaucer Press), Bungay, Suffolk.

# INTRODUCTION

This book is intended to assist students in the early stages of an economics course to understand some of the basic concepts involved in the subject, although it may also prove useful as a revision aid. Experience has shown that students frequently have difficulty at the outset where the issues are clouded by an excess of data and empirical results, although this is essential at a later stage. The objective here is therefore to produce a concise text which explains in simple terms the concepts involved. Having understood these concepts they should utilise other texts which take a more empirical approach, or the text could be supplemented with information provided by the teacher/lecturer during class exercises and data response work. In order to derive the maximum benefit from this book students should first read the companion text Basic Concepts in Micro Economics. This book covers the requirements in Macro Economics for an A level course, but will also be useful to students studying for the foundation stages of professional examinations, first year degree courses, and graduate conversion courses.

*Neil Fuller*

## CARTOONS BY GRAHAM DAVIES

# CONTENTS

# Chapter 1
# NATIONAL INCOME

1.  National income refers to the aggregate, or total, income of the nation which results from economic activity. Income however depends upon how much output is produced and as output is a continuous process rather than a stock, we have to measure this output over a specified time period, usually one year. Total output is referred to as **NATIONAL PRODUCT**, and includes all the **GOODS** and **SERVICES** produced each year.

2.  National income was defined by Alfred Marshall as "the aggregate net product of and sole source of payment to, all the agents of production." If this definition is studied closely we can identify three components:

    2.1   Aggregate net product of, i.e. total output.
    2.2   Sole source of payment, i.e. incomes.
    2.3   All the agents of production, i.e. how the national product is distributed, and therefore the source of all expenditure.

3.  From this definition we can identify three possible methods of measurement:

    3.1   **OUTPUT**
    3.2   **INCOME**
    3.3   **EXPENDITURE.**

Measurement by either of these methods will produce identical results because theoretically:

**NATIONAL INCOME = NATIONAL OUTPUT =**
**NATIONAL EXPENDITURE**

4.  In order to understand the concept of income as a **FLOW** it is useful to study the **CIRCULAR FLOW OF INCOME** in the form of a **FLOW DIAGRAM.** If Diagram 1.1 is studied closely it can be seen that households provide the supply of productive services to firms and in return receive the factor rewards of wages, rent, interest and profit. These are the total of all incomes to households and will therefore form the basis of all expenditures. When expenditures are made with firms in the form of consumption then there must be an

equivalent flow of goods and services from firms to households. It is therefore possible to measure each of these flows and achieve the same result, hence the conclusion that National Income = National Output = National Expenditure. In reality the circular flow Diagram 1.1 needs to be highly qualified, for example much of national expenditure is in the form of investment expenditure between firms, however it does illustrate the concept of national income as a **FLOW**.

DIAGRAM 1.1

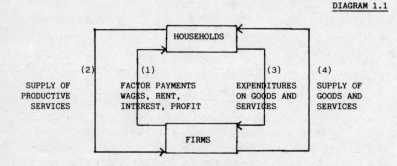

5.   To summarise therefore national income can be regarded as:

5.1   **The tótal value of the goods and services produced by all the industries and public services during the year.**

5.2   **The total expenditure on final goods and services for CONSUMPTION AND INVESTMENT purposes during the year.**

5.3   **The cost of national output in terms of all the earnings: in producing the national output.**

6.   National income is estimated in money terms as money is the most convenient 'measuring rod', however care must be taken in comparing national income over time as a rise in the monetary value of national income does not necessarily imply a rise in living standards. The only real measure of whether national income has grown is whether the **REAL** value of output has increased, and it is possible that any apparent increase is a result of rising prices. For this reason data must be 'deflated' by a suitable index before comparisons of national income between different time periods can be made. One method of deflating data is to use the Retail Price Index.

$$\frac{\text{NATIONAL INCOME AT CURRENT PRICES}}{\text{RPI}} \times 100$$

This method produces national income at **CONSTANT PRICES.** If the index was based on prices in 1975, i.e. 1975 = 100 then the index could be said to be 'at 1975 prices'. As inflation has been removed from the data comparisons over time become more meaningful. National Income and Expenditure (The Blue Book) presents national income data in both current and constant prices.

7. Gross **NATIONAL** Product (GNP) and Gross **DOMESTIC** Product (GDP) differ because some output produced within the U.K. is produced by foreign owned firms and the profits and interest are paid abroad to the owners. Similarly some productive resources overseas are owned by U.K. residents and the profits and interest are remitted back to them. The difference between payments made abroad and payments received from abroad is referred to as **NET PROPERTY INCOME FROM ABROAD** and constitutes the difference between GNP and GDP. Gross **DOMESTIC** product as the name suggests, refers to the output of all domestically (i.e. U.K.) **LOCATED** resources, whilst GNP is the output of all resources **OWNED** by U.K. residents, i.e.:

**GROSS NATIONAL PRODUCT =**
**GROSS DOMESTIC PRODUCT +**
**NET PROPERTY INCOME FROM ABROAD**

**N.B. DOMESTIC PRODUCT** is output produced **WITHIN THE U.K.**

8. During the course of production assets become worn out and require replacement. This is referred to as **CAPITAL CONSUMPTION** or more commonly, **DEPRECIATION.** This is a cost which must be incorporated within national income accounting and is deducted from Gross National Product to obtain the **NET NATIONAL PRODUCT**; also referred to as the **NATIONAL INCOME** i.e.

     **Gross National Product**
less   **Depreciation**
=   **NET NATIONAL PRODUCT = NATIONAL INCOME**

9.  We can now consider the three methods of estimation separately.

9.1  **THE EXPENDITURE METHOD.** This method measures the total amount of **FINAL** expenditures in the course of a year. It includes

  (i)   Consumer's expenditure on goods and services.
 (ii)   Investment expenditure by firms.
(iii)   Additions to stocks are included as **NOMINAL** expenditure.
 (iv)   Expenditure by public authorities on goods and services.

A number of adjustments must be made to the data in order to arrive at the final figure:

(a)   Because the data collected is at **MARKET PRICES** a number of adjustments have to be made in order to find the **FACTOR COST,** i.e. market prices may be distorted by **TAXES** and **SUBSIDIES,** and may not reflect the true cost. As subsidies artificially reduce the market price they are added back on, and as indirect taxes raise the price they are deducted, i.e.

**FACTOR COST = MARKET PRICE + SUBSIDIES**
**— INDIRECT TAXES**

(b)   An adjustment has to be made for the sale of output abroad (exports) and the purchase of goods from abroad (imports).

The Expenditure method of calculation is therefore:

|        |                                                             |
|--------|-------------------------------------------------------------|
|        | Consumers' Expenditure                                      |
| Plus   | Public Authorities' current expenditure on goods and services |
| Plus   | Gross capital formation (investment) at home including increases in stocks |
| =      | Total Domestic Expenditure at market prices                 |
| Plus   | Exports and Income from abroad                               |
| Less   | Imports and Income paid abroad                              |
| Less   | Taxes on expenditure                                        |
| Plus   | Subsidies                                                   |
| =      | GROSS NATIONAL PRODUCT AT FACTOR COST                       |
| Less   | Capital consumption (Depreciation)                          |
| =      | NATIONAL INCOME                                             |

9.2 **THE OUTPUT METHOD**. This method measures the total output of all consumer goods and services, and investment goods, produced by all the firms in the country during the year. This measure can be obtained by totalling the **FINAL** goods and services produced, or by taking the totals of **VALUE ADDED**.

For example, imagine a firm which mines nitrates and sells the crude product to a chemical extracting company at £80 per ton. After refining it is sold to a fertiliser company at £100 per ton who produce and package garden fertiliser for sale to the retail trade at £150 per ton. The retailer sells it to his retail customers at the equivalent of £250 per ton. This is represented diagrammatically in Diagram 1.2 below.

DIAGRAM 1.2

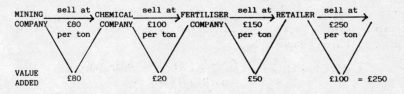

It should be noted that the sum of the value added (£250) is the same as the value of retail sales. Therefore **EITHER** the value of the final goods **OR** the total of value added can be used. What **CANNOT** be done is to add the value of output at each stage because this would involve counting the same item more than once, i.e. the £100 to the fertiliser manufacturer includes the £80 to the mining company. This error is referred to as **DOUBLE COUNTING** and can be a serious source of error in national income accounting.

(b) The output of all industry is classified according to the official Standard Industrial Classification (SIC) and is added together to obtain total output.

(c) A number of 'adjustments' have to be made to the output figures:

    (i) Artificial increases in stock values due to inflation (stock appreciation) have to be deducted.

    (ii) Net property income from abroad.

(iii)   The 'residual error'. In theory the three methods must balance, but in reality they may differ due to errors and delays in returns; the residual error is added to ensure that they do balance. The source of some of these errors is found later and the figures are adjusted in subsequent years.

(d)   **The Output Method**

|  |  |
|---|---|
|  | Agriculture, Forestry and Fishing |
| Plus | Mining and Quarrying |
| Plus | Manufacturing |
| Plus | Construction |
| Plus | Gas, Electricity and Water |
| Plus | Transport |
| Plus | Communication |
| Plus | Distributive trades |
| Plus | Insurance, Banking and Finance |
| Plus | Public Administration and Defence |
| Plus | Public Health and Educational Services |
| Plus | Other Services |
| Plus | Ownership of Dwellings |
|  | Total Domestic Output |
| Less | Stock Appreciation |
| Plus/Minus | Residual Error |
|  | Net Property Income from Abroad |
|  | Gross National Product at Factor Cost |
| Less | Capital Consumption |
| = | NATIONAL INCOME |

## 9.3   THE INCOME METHOD

(a)   This method measures the total money value of all incomes received by persons and firms in the country during the year. These incomes may be in the form of wages, salaries, rent or profit.

(b)   Care must be taken to exclude **TRANSFER PAYMENTS** such as student grants, pensions and unemployment benefit. These are excluded because they do not represent payment for a contribution to output but are transfers of income from one group to another.

(c)   Adjustment has to be made for the undistributed profits of companies and the surpluses of the Nationalised Industries which are paid to the government.

(d)  Adjustments also have to be made for stock appreciation and net property income from abroad.

The Income Method of calculation is therefore:

|            |                                        |
|------------|----------------------------------------|
|            | Income from Employment                 |
| Plus       | Income from Self Employment            |
| Plus       | Profits of private companies and Public Enterprises |
| Plus       | Rent                                   |
| =          | Total Domestic Income                  |
| Less       | Stock Appreciation                     |
| Plus/Minus | Residual Error                         |
| Plus/Minus | Net Property Income from Abroad        |
| =          | Gross National Product                 |
| Less       | Capital Consumption (Depreciation)     |
| =          | NATIONAL INCOME                        |

10.  A number of problems are encountered in the calculation of national income, the main ones being:

10.1  The problem of **DOUBLE COUNTING** (see 9.2 above).

10.2  **TRANSFER PAYMENTS** (see 9.3 above).

10.3  Underestimates may occur where goods and services do not enter the market and are therefore unrecorded. For example goods consumed by those producing them, as is the case with farmers; or farm labourers who receive part of their income in kind.

10.4  Unpaid personal services, e.g. the work of housewives. Housework is an indirect contribution to output in that it enables others in the family to make a more direct contribution.

10.5  Data collection may be inadequate due to firms failing to send in returns or making errors. Also much of the information is originally collected for different purposes, e.g. tax returns.

10.6  The growth of the 'black economy'; in recent years it has been suggested that as much as $7\frac{1}{2}\%$ of GDP may go unrecorded. The 'black economy' refers to that part of economic activity which is undeclared and therefore unrecorded for tax purposes, and is therefore deemed to be 'illegal'. Research suggests that there has been considerable growth in this sector over recent years.

11.   **INTERNATIONAL COMPARISONS** of national income as a basis for comparing 'standards of living' is subject to a number of qualifications:

11.1   Whether or not a particular level of national income implies a high material standard of living also depends upon population size, and measurement requires an estimate of **PER CAPITA** income i.e.

$$\frac{\text{NNP AT FACTOR COST}}{\text{POPULATION}} = \frac{\text{PER CAPITA}}{\text{INCOME}}$$

Therefore the growth of NNP must be greater than population growth in order for living standards to rise.

11.2   'Standard of living' is a subjective evaluation and other nations may put more value upon non material aspects which do not enter national income accounting.

11.3   Climatic differences may mean that although national income may be lower in some countries they have to spend less on fuel and clothing to keep warm.

11.4   Transport in large countries where there are dispersed centres of population may absorb a higher proportion of national income.

11.5   The use of exchange rates to convert national income statistics into a common currency unit may produce unreliable results for comparison purposes.

12.   Whether or not an increase in national income is the same thing as an increase in welfare is a matter of some discussion as national income measurements fail to include factors which many would suggest were an essential aspect of 'welfare', but which cannot be measured purely in terms of material goods. In particular they would indicate:

12.1   'Externalities' such as environmental pollution which may actually become worse as the rate of growth of national income increases.

12.2   The level of provision of 'merit' goods such as education, health and welfare.

12.3 The production of 'demerit' goods such as alcohol and tobacco.

12.4 The level of provision of government transfers such as pensions, grants and social security benefits which are specifically excluded from the statistics in order to avoid double counting, but it could be argued that they cannot be omitted from any measure of welfare.

13. National Income measurements do provide however an indication of whether of not output, and therefore incomes, is rising, and provided the qualifications are borne in mind during interpretation they do provide a useful indication of the trends in the economy.

14. Page 9 shows National Income statistics for the U.K. 1981 measured by each of the three methods.


## SELF ASSESSMENT QUESTIONS

1. What is meant by the circular flow of income?

2. State the three methods by which national income can be calculated.

3. How does the problem of 'double counting' occur?

4. What are 'transfer payments'?

5. Outline the problems which occur in making international comparisons of national income.

6. Describe in detail one method of national income calculation.

# U.K. NATIONAL INCOME 1981 (millions £)

## INCOME

| | |
|---|---:|
| Income from employment | 147,197 |
| Income from self employment | 18,569 |
| Gross trading profits of companies | 27,101 |
| Gross trading surplus of public corporations | 7,551 |
| Gross trading surplus of general government enterprises | 242 |
| Rent | 15,282 |
| Imputed charge for consumption of non trading capital | 2,318 |
| Total Domestic Income | 218,260 |
| Less Stock Appreciation | − 5,692 |
| Residual Error | − 1,780 |
| Gross Domestic Product | 210,788 |
| Net property income from abroad | 1,004 |
| Gross National Product | 211,792 |
| Less Capital Consumption | −30,613 |
| National Income (Net National Product) | 181,179 |

## OUTPUT

| | |
|---|---:|
| Agriculture, forestry and fishing | 4,867 |
| Petroleum and natural gas | 11,972 |
| Other mining and quarrying | 3,455 |
| Manufacturing | 49,916 |
| Construction | 13,545 |
| Gas, electricity and water | 6,670 |
| Transport | 10,935 |
| Communication | 5,858 |
| Distributive trades | 20,088 |
| Insurance, banking and finance | 19,251 |
| Ownership of dwellings | 13,869 |
| Professional and scientific services | 28,467 |
| Miscellaneous services | 20,057 |
| Public administration and defence | 15,988 |
| Total | 224,938 |
| Adjustment for financial services | −12,370 |
| Residual Error | − 1,780 |
| Gross domestic product at factor cost | 210,788 |
| Net Property Income from abroad | 1,004 |
| Gross National Product at factor cost | 211,792 |
| Less Capital Consumption | −30,613 |
| National Income (Net National Product) | 181,179 |

## EXPENDITURE

| | |
|---|---:|
| Consumers' expenditure | 151,042 |
| General government final consumption | 55,151 |
| Gross domestic fixed capital formation | 39,377 |
| Value of physical increase in stock and work in progress | −4,160 |
| Total domestic expenditure | 241,410 |
| Exports of goods and services | 67,854 |
| Total final expenditure | 309,264 |
| Less imports of goods and services | −60,866 |
| Gross domestic product at market prices | 248,398 |
| Net property income from abroad | 1,004 |
| Gross national product at market prices | 249,402 |
| Less Taxes on expenditure | 43,471 |
| Subsidies | 5,861 |
| Gross National Product at Factor Cost | 211,792 |
| Less Capital Consumption | −30,613 |
| National Income (Net National Product) | 181,179 |

SOURCE: National Income and Expenditure 1982

# Chapter 2
# INTERNATIONAL TRADE

1.  Nations engage in international trade for a variety of reasons:

1.1  Due to climatic differences some goods would not be available in many parts of the world without trade. For example, coffee grows prolifically between the tropics, but not elsewhere. This is true of many natural commodities.

1.2  Natural resources are not evenly distributed throughout the world, for example many countries have no coal or oil reserves whilst others have a surplus over their domestic requirements.

1.3  Skills and technology are also not distributed evenly and whilst some countries have a high level of technological development others have a much lower level, both will therefore tend to produce goods of a different nature.

1.4  Because factors of production and natural resources tend to be immobile it is more convenient to specialise in the production of those goods in which there is a natural, or acquired advantage, and trade the surplus not required for domestic consumption for those goods which cannot be produced.

2.  Although it was stated above that certain crops would not grow naturally in some regions of the world, it is not true that they could not be grown given sufficient diversion of resources to their production. For example, bananas can be grown quite successfully in heated greenhouses in the U.K., but the cost would be very high and therefore the output would only be available to the wealthiest people. It is far more efficient for each country to use its resources in the production of those goods in which they have a cost advantage and trade with other nations to obtain those goods which are not produced. For example, the U.K. has an advantage over the West Indies in the production of machinery whilst the West Indies for climatic reasons can grow an abundance of bananas. It is therefore more efficient for Britain to **SPECIALISE** in the production of machines and trade with the West Indies for bananas. Both countries then enjoy the **GAINS FROM TRADE** which result from **SPECIALISATION**.

3. Specialisation and trade increase world output and enables everybody to enjoy a higher standard of living than would be otherwise available. A wider variety of goods are made available to more people.

4. The **LAW OF COMPARATIVE COSTS** shows that countries can gain from specialisation and trade provided that there is some difference in the **RELATIVE COSTS** of producing those goods. The **OPPORTUNITY COST** of producing a good domestically may be too high, for example the growing of bananas in the U.K. quoted above.

5. To illustrate the law of comparative costs, suppose there are two countries X and Y. Both produce just two goods, beef and cars. Both countries have an equivalent amount of capital and labour but X has abundant grasslands and suitable climate for beef production whilst Y has less favourable climate and agricultural conditions but a more highly skilled workforce. There are no unemployed factors in either country. When both countries are using their resources equally to produce **BOTH** goods output is as follows:

| COUNTRY | BEEF (units) | CARS (units) |
|---|---|---|
| X | 1000 | 200 |
| Y | 200 | 1000 |
| TOTAL PRODUCTION BEFORE SPECIALISATION | 1200 | 1200 |

6. If however each country specialises in the production of those goods at which they are most efficient i.e. X specialises in beef and Y in cars, then output is as follows:

| COUNTRY | BEEF (units) | CARS (units) |
|---|---|---|
| X | 2000 | |
| Y | | 2000 |
| TOTAL OUTPUT AFTER SPECIALISATION | 2000 | 2000 |

(Note: It was originally assumed that each country was using half of its resources in the production of each good, therefore if country X could produce 1000 units with half its resources logically it could produce 2000 with all its resources.)

The **NET GAINS** from specialisation are 800 units of beef and 800 units of cars (note: in specialising X gave up the production of 200 cars and Y the production of 200 beef leaving a **NET** gain of 800 of each). In this example each country specialised in the production of goods in which they had a **COMPARATIVE ADVANTAGE.**

7.   If one country is more efficient in the production of **BOTH** goods i.e. has an **ABSOLUTE ADVANTAGE** then it may still be worthwhile engaging in trade if one country specialises in the production of those goods in which its disadvantage is least; referred to as **LEAST COMPARATIVE DISADVANTAGE,** and the other country those goods in which the **COMPARATIVE ADVANTAGE IS GREATEST.**

8.   Suppose that country X was more efficient in the production of both beef and cars, and the positions before specialisation is as follows:

| COUNTRY | BEEF (units) | CARS (units) |
|---|---|---|
| X | 1000 | 600 |
| Y | 800 | 200 |
| TOTAL PRODUCTION BEFORE SPECIALISATION | 1800 | 800 |

Specialisation is still worthwhile as X's comparative advantage is greatest in car production, i.e. three times as efficient, whereas X is only $1\frac{1}{4}$ times more efficient in the production of beef. Therefore if X specialises in cars and Y in beef total production will be as follows:

| COUNTRY | BEEF (units) | CARS (units) |
|---|---|---|
| X | NIL | 1200 |
| Y | 1600 | NIL |
| TOTAL PRODUCTION AFTER SPECIALISATION | 1600 | 1200 |

If demand and supply on world markets dictate that 2 units of beef are the equivalent of 1 car Y can trade 800 units of beef for 400 cars and after specialisation and trade country X has 800 units of beef and 800 cars and country Y has 800 beef and 400 cars. X is better off by 200 cars (the equivalent of 400 beef) and Y is better off by 200 cars and has the same amount of beef. World output in **VALUE** terms has risen.

9. Trade will continue as long as the **DOMESTIC OPPORTUNITY COST RATIOS IN THE TWO COUNTRIES ARE DIFFERENT.** Trade would cease when it cost more in terms of resources for X to import beef than to produce it. If X could produce beef more cheaply in terms of cars than Y by transferring resources to beef production then trade would cease.

10. Trade theory must be qualified however to allow for the fact that there may be some loss of efficiency when transferring production from one good to another. Also, transport costs will be incurred, which may outweigh a marginal cost advantage.

11. **THE TERMS OF TRADE** refer to the rate at which one nation's goods can be exchanged for those of others. In the example above it was 2:1. In reality physical goods are not exchanged but prices are paid in various currencies. The terms of trade are measured by means of a **TERMS OF TRADE INDEX** which is calculated as:

$$\frac{\textbf{INDEX OF EXPORT PRICES}}{\textbf{INDEX OF IMPORT PRICES}} \times \textbf{100}$$

The base year of the index is 100. An improvement in the terms of trade is said to be **FAVOURABLE** and shows as an increase in the index, indicating that a given volume of exports can be exchanged for a greater volume of imports. A fall in the index is said to be **UNFAVOURABLE** as a given volume of exports can only be exchanged for a smaller volume of imports. The terms of trade index has important implications for the U.K.'s performance as a trading nation.

Table 2.1 shows the U.K. Terms of Trade 1973-1983.

TABLE 2.1

| YEAR | TERMS OF TRADE (1980=100) |
|------|---------------------------|
| 1973 | 97.7 |
| 1974 | 81.5 |
| 1975 | 87.8 |
| 1976 | 85.8 |
| 1977 | 87.7 |
| 1978 | 92.8 |
| 1979 | 96.4 |
| 1980 | 100.0 |
| 1981 | 101.0 |
| 1982 | 99.3 |
| 1983 | 98.5 |

SOURCE: ECONOMIC TRENDS

12.   Despite the gains from free international trade nations have frequently attempted to restrict the amount of trade in order to protect their domestic economies from the effects of foreign competition. This competition may be from lower cost producers due to either, or both, greater efficiency and lower wage costs. Such an attitude is referred to as **"PROTECTIONISM"** and restrictions on trade may take a variety of forms:

12.1   Tariffs — taxes on imports, generally referred to as duties.

12.2   Quotas — physical limits on the quantities of specified goods which can be imported.

12.3   Subsidies — to domestic producers to reduce their prices below those of foreign competitors.

12.4   Exchange Control Regulations — limit the amount of foreign currency available to pay for imports.

12.5    Physical Controls — a complete ban or embargo.

13.    The arguments generally put forward in favour of restrictions on trade are:

13.1    To protect a new or developing industry — the 'infant industry case'.

13.2    To assist in the elimination of a balance of payments deficit.

13.3    To protect the domestic economy against unemployment caused by too many imported goods.

13.4    To protect strategically important industries such as iron, steel and shipbuilding.

13.5    To protect the domestic economy from 'unfair' competition, in particular 'dumping' where excess production is sold abroad at cost in order to cover fixed costs only, and allow profits to be made on the domestic market; or where 'cheap' labour is being used (e.g. child labour).

14.    Protecting domestic industries from competition in order to ensure their survival is a dubious argument. In the long run protection from competition results in a loss of efficiency and inventiveness, and when eventually industries have to face international competition again they will be weak and ill-equipped to do so.

15.    The costs of protection however are generally borne by consumers who are forced to pay higher prices and have a restricted choice of goods. Also, trade is possibly the best way of forging links between countries and promoting international co-operation. Attempts to interfere with trade generally result in some form of retaliation which may lead to a disastrous trade war where everybody loses.

16.    It cannot be assumed that because a country has a comparative advantage in the production of a particular good that it will retain that advantage indefinitely. The centres of comparative advantage in production tend to change over time, particularly with changes in technology and the growth of capital resources, for example, Britain's comparative advantage in the production of cotton textiles has shifted towards the cotton producing countries. Changes in comparative advantage can be a major cause of **STRUCTURAL UNEMPLOYMENT** (see Chapter 5).

## SELF ASSESSMENT QUESTIONS

1. Distinguish between an absolute and a comparative advantage.

2. What are the gains from trade?

3. What are the 'terms of trade'?

4. How is the 'terms of trade index' calculated?

5. Why might nations impose restrictions on trade?

# Chapter 3
# BALANCE OF PAYMENTS

1.   The balance of payments in the accounting sense is a record of all the transactions of the U.K. with the rest of the world. Like all accounting balance sheets the balance of payments taken as a whole **MUST** be in balance, what is more important however is the performance in the component sections.

2.   Table 3.1 illustrates the Summary Balance of Payments Accounts for the U.K. for 1981.

TABLE 3.1

|  | £mn |
|---|---|
| VISIBLE BALANCE (TRADE BALANCE) | +3652 |
| INVISIBLE BALANCE | +3620 |
| | |
| CURRENT BALANCE | +7272 |
| Investment and Other Transactions | −7194 |
| Balancing Item | − 765 |
| | |
| BALANCE FOR OFFICIAL FINANCING | −687 |
| Other Transactions & Official | |
| Borrowing | −1732 |
| Drawings on (+) Additions to (−) | |
| Official Reserves | +2419 |
| | |
| TOTAL OFFICIAL FINANCING | + 687 |

The figures shown are net figures i.e. the figure after imports (inflows) are offset by corresponding exports (outflows).

3.   The part of the accounts which receives most attention is the **CURRENT BALANCE.** The current balance has two components, **VISIBLES** and **INVISIBLES**.

3.1   The **VISIBLE BALANCE** comprises of the import and export of **GOODS**. Until the 1980's Britain rarely had a surplus on visibles, however since the advent of North Sea Oil a surplus on visible trade has been regularly achieved.

3.2  **INVISIBLES** refers to trade services and to transfers. These include:

(a)  Shipping.
(b)  Civil Aviation.
(c)  Insurance.
(d)  Banking.
(e)  Tourism.
(f)  Interest and Profits.
(g)  Government transfers e.g. military and diplomatic expenditure.
(h)  Private Transfers.

3.3  Britain has generally had a substantial surplus on invisible trade, sufficient to outweigh the deficit on visibles. Although on occasion the deficit on trade has been so great that even after allowing for invisibles there was a substantial **DEFICIT ON CURRENT ACCOUNT**. Table 3.2 illustrates how a trade deficit can become a current account surplus after the inclusion of invisibles.

TABLE 3.2

|  | £mn |
|---|---|
| VISIBLE TRADE | |
| Exports | 2500 |
| Imports | 3300 |
| Trade Deficit | - 800 |
| | |
| INVISIBLE TRADE | |
| Exports | 1900 |
| Imports | 1000 |
| Invisible Surplus | + 900 |
| | |
| CURRENT ACCOUNT SURPLUS | + 100 |

4.  The current account is generally taken as being the main indicator of the nation's performance in international trade.

5.  **INVESTMENT AND OTHER CAPITAL TRANSACTIONS** refers to various types of capital inflows and outflows. They include overseas investment in the U.K., deposits with banks and other financial institutions, and the allocation of Special Drawing Rights (SDR's) and gold subscriptions to the IMF.

A deficit on current account may be offset by a surplus on Investment and Other Capital Transactions. This may imply however, an increase in future outflows when the remittance of profits and interest overseas have to be made.

6.   The sum of Current Balance and Investment and Other Capital Transactions gives the Balance for Official Financing. This constitutes the total inflow or outflow of currency to or from the U.K. and therefore shows the net amount which the authorities will either have to finance from the reserves if it is negative, or pay into the reserves (or use to repay earlier loans) if it is positive.

7.   **TOTAL OFFICIAL FINANCING** shows how the authorities either financed the deficit or disposed of the surplus and will therefore be of exactly the same size as the Balance for Official Financing, but of opposite sign. If there was a surplus on the Balance for Official Financing, Official Financing shows how it was disposed of, if there was a deficit is shows how it was financed. Deficits may be financed by either drawing on the reserves (shown as a +) or borrowing from other central banks, or from the International Monetary Fund (shown also as a +). Payments into the reserves or repayments are shown as negative.

8.   The sum of the Current Balance and Investment and Other Capital Transactions must in theory be equal to the Total Official Financing, a figure which is known with a reasonable degree of accuracy. In reality however, due to various errors and omissions, it may not be equal, so a **BALANCING ITEM** is added to make them balance. Eventually the source of some of the errors is found and the adjustments to the accounts made later.

9.   Reference to **EQUILIBRIUM** or **DISEQUILIBRIUM** in the balance of payments usually refers to the **CURRENT ACCOUNT**. Equilibrium is generally taken to refer to the fact that exports are equal to imports. This definition has to be qualified however, and before it is truly meaningful should include discussion of:

    (i) The time period involved.
    (ii) The exchange rate — if the exchange rate is freely floating then equilibrium in the balance of payments will always be attained.
    (iii) The exchange rate may be managed in order to manipulate transactions in such a way as to make them balance.

10.   A deficit in the balance of payments means that in the short run the nation is enjoying a higher material standard of living than it would otherwise do. Such a situation can however only be maintained for as long as there are adequate reserves. In the absence of bottomless reserves no country can run a balance of payments deficit indefinitely.

11.   Policies to correct a balance of payments deficit include:

11.1   A reduction in the exchange rate to make exports cheaper and imports dearer (see Chapter 4).

11.2   Import controls — may result in 'retaliation'.

11.3   Expenditure 'dampening  policies' — reducing the level of domestic demand for all goods including imports. This has high costs in terms of domestic output and therefore employment.

11.4   Expenditure 'switching policies', intended to shift domestic expenditure from imports to domestically produced goods. An example here is raising the price of imports relative to domestic goods by imposing duties.

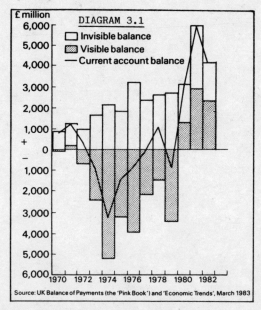

SOURCE: ECONOMIC PROGRESS REPORT NO. 157

11.5 Subsidies or aid to exporters.

11.6 Increasing the domestic rate of interest in order to attract capital inflows.

12. Diagram 3.1 illustrates Britain's Balance of Payments 1970 to 1982.

## SELF ASSESSMENT QUESTIONS

1. Distinguish between visibles and invisibles.

2. How is the current balance obtained?

3. Does a deficit on the balance of payments necessarily imply a reduction in the standard of livi⁻g of the nation?

4. How is the Total Currency Flow obtained?

5. In what ways may a deficit on the balance of payments be financed?

# Chapter 4
# EXCHANGE RATES

1. The Exchange Rate refers to the rate at which one currency can be exchanged for another, e.g. pounds for deutschmarks, or dollars. As we are discussing how many dollars etc. we can obtain for a pound then it is the same as discussing the **PRICE** of foreign currency. In the rest of this discussion reference will be made only to the rate of exchange between dollars and pounds (sterling), there are of course rates of exchange between all currencies and the analysis of them is identical.

2. Exchange rates are important because they determine the prices at which U.K. goods will be sold abroad, and the price at which foreign goods will be sold in the U.K. They therefore have a direct effect on the balance of payments and the domestic economy.

3. If the exchange rate between pounds and dollars was originally £1 = $2, and then on the international market began to be exchanged at £1 = $1.50 we would refer to a **FALL** in the **VALUE OF THE POUND** relative to the dollar, and the price of U.K. goods selling in America in dollar prices would fall. If the rate of exchange became £1 = $2.50 we would refer to a **RISE** in the **VALUE OF THE POUND** relative to the dollar and the dollar price of U.K. goods in America would rise.

4. As mentioned above, the exchange rate is really the price of foreign currency and as is the case with other goods, price is determined by supply and demand. In the absence of intervention by governments therefore, exchange rates are determined by the demand for, and supply of, currencies. The price of the pound in terms of the dollar will depend upon the demand for the pound by holders of dollars and the supply of pounds will be from holders of pounds who want to buy dollars. The demand for pounds is derived from the demand by overseas residents for British goods and who require pounds to pay for them. The supply of pounds is derived from the demand by U.K. residents for goods from overseas and who require foreign currency to pay for them. In exchanging pounds for foreign currency, in this case dollars, the supply of pounds is increased. The demand for, and supply of, pounds takes place on the

FOREIGN EXCHANGE MARKETS, and the EQUILIBRIUM EXCHANGE RATE will be where demand and supply are equal. In diagram 4.1 the equilibrium exchange rate is where the demand and supply for sterling are equal. Clearly the value of a nation's currency depends ultimately upon its overseas trade performance. A balance of payments surplus would therefore indicate a high demand for pounds in order to pay for U.K. goods, the exchange rate would therefore be high relative to other currencies. A deficit would imply an excess supply of pounds and a weak currency.

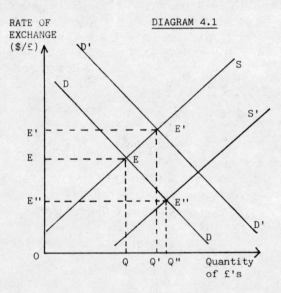

5. In diagram 4.1 the shift in the demand for sterling from DD to D'D' has caused an increase in the equilibrium exchange rate relative to dollars from E to E'. Such a shift could be caused by:

5.1 An increased preference amongst U.S. citizens for British goods.

5.2 An increase in incomes in the United States.

6. An increase in imports into the U.K. from the U.S.A. would increase the supply of pounds, shown in diagram 4.1 as the shift in the supply curve from SS to S'S', with a consequent reduction in the equilibrium exchange rate from E to E''.

7.   A fall in the value of the pound will, ceteris paribus:

   7.1   Raise the price of imports.
   7.2   Reduce the price of exports.

An increase in the value of the pound will, ceteris paribus:

   7.3   Reduce the price of imports.
   7.4   Raise the price of exports.

8.   **PURCHASING POWER PARITY THEORY** explains the equilibrium exchange rate between two currencies in terms of the price levels in the two countries. It states that the value of one currency relative to another depends upon the relative purchasing power of the two currencies in their domestic economies i.e. the exchange rate will be determined at the point where the purchasing power of a unit of the currency is the same in each country. The theory can be expressed as follows:

$$\text{The price of the pound in dollars} = \frac{\textbf{U.S. Price Level}}{\textbf{U.K. Price Level}}$$

This has important implications for the relationship between exchange rates and inflation. Although short-run deviations from purchasing power parity are possible, in the long run the theory probably does hold true.

9.   **FLOATING, FREE OR FLEXIBLE EXCHANGE RATES** refer to an exchange rate system such as that described above where the equilibrium rate of exchange is determined by the forces of demand and supply on the foreign exchange market. The following characteristics of floating exchange rates should be borne in mind:

   9.1   A businessman who enters a contract with an overseas supplier for delivery of goods at a future date with payment in foreign currency upon delivery never knows exactly how much he will have to pay as the exchange rate may be subject to fluctuation in the intervening period. Some argue that this tends to act as a deterrent to international trade. It is possible however to safeguard against currency fluctuations by buying currency ahead on the forward exchange market.

   9.2   In a free exchange rate system the action of speculators will tend to stabilise the currency around a long term trend as they buy the currency when it is weak and sell it when it is dear.

9.3 Under a flexible exchange rate system the balance of payments should be self correcting. A deficit resulting in a fall in the exchange rate which reduces the price of U.K. exports and therefore demand increases. At the same time the increase in the price of imports should reduce some of the demand for imports. Eventually balance of payments equilibrium should be re-established.

10. **FIXED EXCHANGE RATE** systems are intended to remove the uncertainty associated with flexible rates. The fixed exchange rate system was introduced at the **Bretton Woods Conference** in 1944 and was effective from 1947. The system was intended to bring stability to world trade and to stimulate its growth. The **International Monetary Fund** was also established in order to assist countries with balance of payments difficulties. The fixed exchange rate system was finally abandoned in 1973.

11. Each currency was given a **PAR VALUE** in terms of the dollar e.g. £1 = $2.80 and the Central Bank of each country (in the U.K. the Bank of England) agreed to intervene on the foreign exchange markets in order to maintain the value of its currency 1% either side of the par value, widened to 2¼% either side of par in 1971. In diagram 4.2 the par value is £1 = $2.40. As a result of an increase in imports the supply of pounds shifts from SS to S'S' and equilibrium shifts to E' with a new exchange rate at $2.00. However the Central

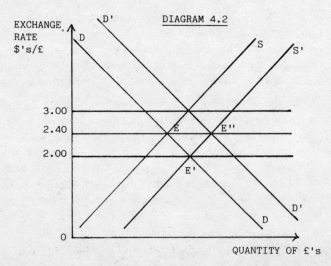

Bank intervenes and buys pounds with gold or foreign currency shifting the demand from DD to D′D′ with a new equilibrium at E″ and the exchange rate returns to par value at $2.40. Had the exchange rate risen to £1 = $3.00 the Bank of England would have intervened and sold pounds in order to increase the supply and return to the par value. An essential component of such a scheme is large reserves of gold and foreign currency. Under the scheme member countries could draw reserves from the IMF for this purpose when their currencies came under pressure.

12.    The major **ADVANTAGE** claimed for fixed exchange rates is that they eliminate uncertainty from international trade.

13.    The alleged **DISADVANTAGES** of fixed exchange rates are:

13.1    If the original rate is set too high i.e. above the equilibrium rate, then it will be difficult to achieve a balance of payments equilibrium.

13.2    Domestic policies for managing the economy are dominated by the need to maintain the external value of the currency.

13.3    Fixed exchange rates are subject to extreme speculative pressures. The speculator has 'everything to gain and little to lose'. If he anticipates a **DEVALUATION** of the sterling exchange rate and sells pounds, this can only add to the pressure for devaluation; after devaluation he can buy the pounds back at a lower rate. Even if the devaluation does not occur he is no worse off. In the event of an anticipated **REVALUATION** the purchase of pounds can only add to the pressure for revaluation, again if it does not come about the speculator has little to lose. The pound came under extreme pressure from speculators in the 1960's and early 1970's when the overvalued pound resulted in a series of balance of payments deficits.

14.    **DEVALUATION** refers to the deliberate reduction of the exchange rate relative to other currencies in a fixed exchange rate system. The objective being to make exports more competitive in terms of foreign currency whilst imports become more expensive. Under the fixed exchange rate system this was allowed where a nation was subject to recurring balance of payments difficulties. The U.K. devalued sterling in 1949 and in 1967. **REVALUATION** refers to the decision to raise the par value of the exchange rate. Devaluation will not necessarily result in an improvement in the balance of payments however.

14.1 If the demand for exports is **INELASTIC** then the devaluation may not raise total export earnings, and the desired improvement in the balance of payments will be even more difficult to achieve if the demand for imports is also **INELASTIC**.

14.2 If other trading nations retaliate with a successive round of devaluations then the advantage gained from the devaluation will soon be lost.

14.3 There must be sufficient excess capacity in the domestic economy to meet the increased demand for exports.

15. The initial impact of a currency depreciation or devaluation may well be to cause a deterioriation in the current account. In a manufacturing economy such as the U.K. this occurs because raw materials have to be imported at a higher cost than previously and in larger quantities if more goods are to be manufactured for export. Eventually the effect of the depreciation results in a higher level of exports, and domestic goods are substituted for imports, the current account then moves into surplus. This effect, known as the **J-CURVE EFFECT**, is illustrated in diagram 4.3.

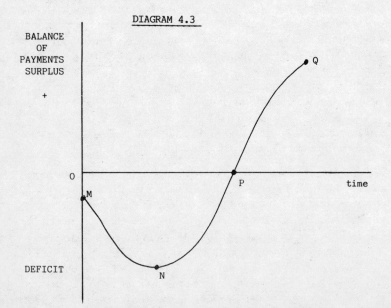

DIAGRAM 4.3

The depreciation at M initially results in a deterioration of the current account. At point N the effect of the depreciation begins to feed through to exports and the current account starts to improve, moving back into surplus at P.

16.  Under a fixed exchange rate system devaluation tends to become confused with issues such as national pride, under a floating rate the exchange rate adjusts automatically to equilibrium with the domestic economy being less sensitive to changes in external demand. Under floating exchange rates a fall in the exchange rate is referred to as a **DEPRECIATION** and an increase in the exchange rate as an **APPRECIATION**.

17.  The devaluation of sterling in 1967 was the first crack in the fixed exchange rate system. Following this other currencies came under successive bouts of speculative pressure, and later with the onset of world recession, inflation, and the oil price crisis of 1973/74, the system became increasingly unstable. Despite various attempts to restore it, in particular the Smithsonian Institute agreement in 1971 and the various attempts to establish a European Monetary System; sterling was allowed to float in June 1972 effectively signalling the end of the Bretton Woods system. Today most exchange rates operate on the basis of what may be referred to as a 'dirty floating' system. There are no agreed intervention points but Central Banks will intervene if they consider that excessive speculative activity is resulting in a depreciation which will harm the domestic economy.

## SELF ASSESSMENT QUESTIONS

1.  Distinguish between fixed and floating exchange rates.

2.  Why was the fixed exchange rate system introduced?

3.  What are the major disadvantages of fixed exchange rates?

4.  Distinguish between a Devaluation and a Depreciation of a currency.

5.  In what circumstances would devaluation result in an improvement in the balance of payments?

# Chapter 5
# UNEMPLOYMENT

1.  **Labour is the least durable of all resources**; a day's output lost due to unemployment is lost permanently and cannot be regained. Unemployment therefore has high economic costs, but in addition the costs in terms of misery and despair cannot be ignored.

2.  In order to formulate appropriate policies to cure unemployment it is necessary to identify precisely the type of unemployment which is being dealt with as the policy instruments appropriate to the cure of one type may not be appropriate to another. It is usual to classify unemployment as one of four types: **SEASONAL, FRICTIONAL, STRUCTURAL** and **CYCLICAL (DEFICIENT DEMAND).**

3.  **SEASONAL UNEMPLOYMENT:** Some industries are highly seasonal in character and the levels of unemployment in such industries therefore also tends to fluctuate with the seasons, e.g. the hotel and catering industry in resorts, fruit picking, and the construction industry.

4.  **FRICTIONAL UNEMPLOYMENT:** This results from the frictions in the labour market which occur due to labour immobility, or the process of searching for job information. Even at what is normally deemed to be full employment there would still be an element of frictional unemployment because it takes time and resources for workers to change jobs. There may be an adequate number of vacancies but it takes time for a suitable match between those seeking employment and appropriate vacancies to be found.

5.  **STRUCTURAL UNEMPLOYMENT:** This type of unemployment arises out of more fundamental changes in the industrial base of the economy. It is associated with the decline of 'staple' industries and the problem arises because as industries decline the skills required for them become obsolete also. This becomes a serious problem because these industries tend to be concentrated in certain **REGIONS** and when these industries decline **REGIONAL DECLINE** occurs as a consequence. Examples include: shipbuilding in the North West, North East, Glasgow and Northern Ireland; cotton textiles in the North West; iron and steel making in

South Wales and the North East, and some of the coal fields in the North West and the North. Vacancies may exist in the economy but they may be in different areas and involve different skills. The concentration of unemployment in the regions becomes a problem due to:

5.1   The occupational immobility of labour — the unwillingness to abandon skills and acquire new ones.

5.2   The geographical immobility of labour — workers are reluctant to move to vacancies elsewhere due to cultural, family and financial ties to the regions. Structural decline may result from some or all of the following:

5.3   Technological change.

5.4   The development of substitutes e.g. the effect of man-made fibres such as nylon on the cotton industry.

5.5   The growth of overseas competition.

DIAGRAM 5.1

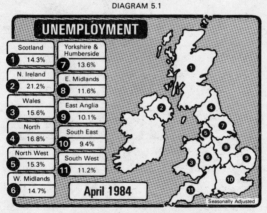

SOURCE: FINANCIAL TIMES 31/3/84

6.   Diagram 5.1 illustrates the regional variation in unemployment rates. The reluctance of labour to move from the regions has resulted in the alternative policy of moving 'work to the workers' in the form of **REGIONAL POLICY**, under which Governments have used a variety of measures in order to encourage firms to expand into the regions of high unemployment. (See chapter 6).

7. **CYCLICAL UNEMPLOYMENT:** This type of unemployment results from a general deficiency of total demand in the economy. (This is dealt with in more detail in Chapter 12.)

8. There were in 1984 three times as many unemployed as there were in the 1950's and there are three further important points to note regarding recent unemployment.

8.1 The increase in unemployment among the young.

8.2 An increase in the duration of unemployment. This can be deduced from the relationship between unemployment and vacancies in Diagram 5.2.

DIAGRAM 5.2

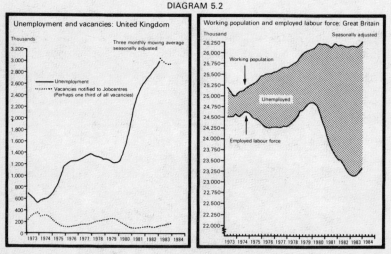

SOURCE: EMPLOYMENT GAZETTE APRIL 1984

8.3 The period of rising unemployment has coincided with an increase in the size of the working population, as can be seen in Diagram 5.2.

9. In February 1984 unemployment in Great Britain (exd. N. Ireland) stood at 3,063.8 million or 13.1% of the working population.

**SELF ASSESSMENT QUESTIONS**

1. How does frictional unemployment occur and why is it a less serious problem than other forms of unemployment?

2. Why does structural unemployment create a problem for the regions?

3. What is meant by Regional Policy and why have governments in the past felt that they needed such a policy?

4. In what sense is unemployment a waste of resources?

# Chapter 6
# REGIONAL POLICY

1. The regional imbalance of incomes and employment which arises from the decline of the staple industries in the regions has resulted in the devising of various measures aimed at reducing these regional disparities. These measures, generally referred to as **REGIONAL POLICY**, attempt to encourage the growth of industry in the regions. Government intervention in this context arises from the desire for the greater economic growth which will result from a fuller utilisation of resources, both labour and capital; and a desire for greater equality of employment and incomes. Because of the reluctance of labour to move to areas of high employment measures generally attempt to influence the firm's location decision i.e. "bring work to the workers", by a combination of measures aimed at reducing the firm's costs if they locate in specified areas or by prohibiting through planning regulations expansion elsewhere (the 'carrot and stick' approach).

2. The present pattern of assistance was established in the 1972 Industry Act, although Regional Policy originated in the 1930's and expanded rapidly in the 1960's. The extent of assistance available varies according to the designation of the area. Prior to November 1984 there were three categories of Development Area:

2.1 SPECIAL DEVELOPMENT AREAS (S.D.A.'s).

2.2 DEVELOPMENT AREAS (D.A.'s).

2.3 INTERMEDIATE AREAS (I.A.'s).

S.D.A.'s were the areas with the most serious problems of structural decline such as Merseyside, Clydeside and Newcastle, and these received the greatest assistance. The scale of assistance was less in the D.A.'s and I.A.'s. Northern Ireland was categorised as a Special Development area, receiving additional assistance because of the unique problems of that region. In November 1984 the category of SPECIAL DEVELOPMENT AREA was dispensed with leaving only two categories for assistance:

2.4 DEVELOPMENT AREAS.

2.5 INTERMEDIATE AREAS.

MAP 6.1

# ASSISTED AREAS

■ Development Areas

▨ Intermediate Areas

GLASGOW

NEWCASTLE

Isles of Scilly

The distribution of the development areas is illustrated in map 6.1.

3. The main instruments of Regional Policy are as follows:

3.1 **REGIONAL DEVELOPMENT GRANTS (R.D.G's).** These are grants payable to firms on plant, machinery, buildings and works. Up to November 1984 they were available at the following rates:

(a)   22% in Special Development Areas.

(b)   15% in Development Areas.

(c)   **NIL** in Intermediate Areas.

Following the abandonment of Special Development Area status in November 1984 the distribution the grants payable are as follows:

(a)   15% in Development Areas.

(b)   **NIL** in Intermediate Areas.

However the old system of grants will be run in tandem with the new until November 1985.

In addition capital grants were made subject to a cost per job limit of £10,000. An alternative, a job grant, was made available of £3,000 for each  new job created in labour intensive projects. Also, the grants were made available to specifed service industries to whom they had been previously denied.

Capital grants have been subject to the criticism that they encourage capital intensive production when the underlying purpose is the creation of jobs. The Special Development Area status was criticised on the grounds that the extra grant merely attracted industry away from neighbouring Development Areas and such movements did little to create any actual increase in jobs; merely creating jobs in one area at the expense of another. The reduction of the grants available to 15% in Development Areas, the cost per job limit, and the job grant, could be considered as going some way towards meeting these criticisms. The measure introduced in November 1984 are estimated to save £300 million per year and represent a significant movement towards a more market orientated approach to regional policy.

3.2   The provision of **'ADVANCE FACTORIES'** for sale or rent on favourable terms or even rent free for a period. These are standard factory units constructed by a division of the Department of Trade and Industry and are immediately available for firms to move into. There has been more emphasis recently on smaller units ('Busybee Workshops') in order to encourage the growth of new businesses.

3.3   **ENTERPRISE ZONES.** These represent an attempt to deal with the problems of the inner cities and go beyond what is strictly regional policy as some of them lie outside the Development Areas. The concept reflects the view held by the present (1984) government that excessive controls and regulations can stifle initiative. The zones are specified areas mainly within the larger cities where special provisions apply in order to encourage industrial and commerical activity. At present there are 22 such zones in areas such as Merseyside (Speke), Midlands (Corby & Dudley), Northern Ireland (Belfast), Greater Manchester (Salford Docks and Trafford Park), Tyneside (Newcastle and Gateshead). The main incentives in the Enterprise Zones are as follows:

(i)　Exemption from Development Land Tax.

(ii)　100% capital allowances (for Corporation and Income Tax purposes) for commercial and industrial buildings.

(iii)　Exemption from rates on industrial and commercial property.

(iv)　Simplified and relaxed regulations for planning procedures.

(v)　Simpler and speedier administration of remaining controls, and government requests for statistical information is to be kept to minimum.

3.4　**REGIONAL SELECTIVE ASSISTANCE.** This is a variety of further grants available for capital and training costs where it can be shown that jobs will be created.

3.5　**INDUSTRIAL DEVELOPMENT CERTIFICATES** (I.D.C.'s). These represent a form of administrative control on industrial development outside the assisted areas. An I.D.C. was originally required for all new factories or extensions, and by refusing to grant an I.D.C. for anywhere outside a development area pressure could be exerted to ensure that development took place within the development areas. The use of I.D.C.'s as a policy instrument has declined during the 1970's and since the onset of recession has been virtually unused due to the fear of stifling any potential development, and also as a consequence of the less interventionist stance taken by government since 1979.

4.　The **EUROPEAN ECONOMIC COMMUNITY (E.E.C.)** also provides regional assistance. The European Regional Development Fund makes loans to central and local government for spending on capital and infrastructure projects. Receipts from the fund are intended to make government spending in the regions higher than it otherwise would be, and are not given to individual firms. Loans may also be available on favourable terms from the European Investment Bank for projects in the regions.

5. The **FREE-MARKET APPROACH** to the regional problem suggests that any interference in the location decisions of firms will lead to location decisions which are non optimal and therefore inefficient. The firm makes its location decision on the basis of cost minimisation and any interference with his process, it is suggested, will result in a location being chosen which is not the best one in terms of economic efficiency.

5.1 Advocates of the free-market approach suggest that the **REGIONAL PROBLEM WILL SOLVE ITSELF IF LEFT TO MARKET FORCES.** Regional unemployment merely indicates a labour market disequilibrium with an excess supply of labour at the prevailing wage rates and all that is required is a reduction in wages which will then be reflected in lower product prices and equilibrium will be re-established in the labour market. Labour and capital should be free to make their own decisions regarding location and if unemployment is high in a region then wage rates will be lower and some labour will be attracted to other more prosperous regions by the higher wage rates. Also at some point in time the lower wage rates in the declining regions will begin to attract firms who realise that by locating there they can reduce their wage costs and ultimately increase their profits. Eventually this movement of labour and capital will re-establish an equilibrium situation with full employment. If labour is unwilling to move then there must be some other advantages which equalize the employment disadvantages, the same is also true of firms who are unwilling to move voluntarily into the regions.

5.2 The market approach is generally advocated by those who believe that government intervention in the market should be minimal if economic efficiency is to be achieved. Advocates of the free-market approach also suggest that there are further burdens imposed by government intervention in the form of taxation, subsidisation, and the imposition of bureaucratic controls.

6. **OPPONENTS OF THE MARKET APPROACH** however point to a number of weaknesses in that principle:

6.1. **THE TIME SCALE INVOLVED** in the re-establishment of a new equilibrium situation may be very lengthy as the comparative advantage in production between regions is likely to change only slowly.

6.2. **SOCIAL COSTS** may be imposed in both the areas of expansion and of contraction. In the declining regions as labour departs there will be costs imposed by the underutilisation of existing factilities such as schools and hospitals which will fall into decline as the regional income falls. In the expanding areas there will be a shortage of such social facilities with a high level of demand for those facilities which do exist. There are also likely to be the problems of inner-city decay and falling property prices in the declining regions, with shortages of accommodation and rapidly rising prices in the areas of growth. There may also be additional costs from congestion as roads and transport facilities are used more intensively in the growth areas.

6.3 The market solution ignores the **HARDSHIP AND SUFFERING IMPOSED** upon those involved, which may be so extreme that governments may find it politically unacceptable.

6.4 As labour leaves the declining region the population falls, reducing the size of the potential market for new firms in the region. The departure of labour and firms also reduces local expenditure, and therefore incomes, resulting in further unemployment in the ancillary industries such as retailing and distribution. This further decline in incomes is referred to as the **REGIONAL MULTIPLIER** and makes it less likely that firms will locate in the declining regions. The opposite is the case in the expanding regions where the regional multiplier sets in train a circle of rising incomes and prosperity and is likely to be a factor in attracting firms to the more prosperous regions.

6.5 The assumption that the labour market operates in a frictionless manner must also be questioned in the light of **NATIONWIDE COLLECTIVE BARGAINING.** Nationwide collective bargaining has the effect of reducing regional wage differences. Where national representatives of a Trade Union negotiate a national wage rate for their membership then the sensitivity of wage rates to regional differences in employment will be reduced.

7. The effectiveness of regional policy is difficult to quantify, however most studies indicate that regional unemployment is worse in the absence of a policy but that the effect has been only marginal, with the creation of between 200,000 and 350,000 jobs over the past two decades at a cost estimated at approximately £50,000 per job. Such measures of the 'cost per job' created are however unrealistic because they fail to include the social costs and benefits involved. Regional differences in employment and income are substantial, and despite the assistance to the regions the position of the South East, which appears to have the comparative advantage in the modern growth industries, has improved relative to the Assisted Areas. With the onset of the general recession in the mid 1970's unemployment in some of the previously prosperous regions such as the West Midlands has risen to match that in the older Development Areas.

8. In reality the choice lies not between the two extreme views of the free market and the planned location approach, but in the selection of the most appropriate mix. In recent years less emphasis has been placed on regional policy with a move towards a more market-orientated solution. There is however still an important role for the policy for the regions.

## SELF ASSESSMENT QUESTIONS

1. Why is there a 'regional problem'?

2. What are the main instruments of U.K. Regional Policy?

3. Outline the market approach to the regional problem.

4. What are the main problems involved with the market approach to the regional problem?

# Chapter 7

# TAXATION

1. Taxes were originally levied for the purposes of raising **REVENUE**, in a modern economy however they are also used as a means of regulating the level of total (aggregate) demand (see Chapter 12), redistributing incomes and wealth, and regulating markets.

2. Adam Smith stated that the four 'canons' (principles) of taxation were as follows:

2.1 **EQUITY**

2.2 **CERTAINTY**

2.3 **EFFICIENCY**

2.4 **CONVENIENCE**

3. **EQUITY** referred to the principle that taxes should generally be seen to be fair.

4. **CERTAINTY** refers to the principle that the taxpayer should know his tax liability in advance and that the government should know their revenue in advance.

5. **EFFICIENCY** refers to the principle that a good tax will be economic to administer and the costs of administration should be a small proportion of the tax revenue.

6. **CONVENIENCE** refers to the principle that taxes should be levied at a time and place convenient to the taxpayer.

7. In a modern economy there are a number of additional criteria for an efficient tax system.

7.1 **NEUTRALITY** — Taxes should as far as possible be neutral, i.e. not distort the price mechanism. The way in which resources were allocated prior to the introduction of the tax should be the same afterwards. Direct taxation is generally held to be superior in terms of neutrality than indirect taxation. The cost to the economy in terms of resource misallocation, which is incurred as a consequence of indirect taxation, is referred to as other **EXCESS BURDEN** of indirect taxation. The excess burden is greatest the more indirect taxes change the **RELATIVE PRICES** of goods.

7.2 **STABILISATION** — Taxes should be efficient from the point of view of their use in regulating the level of aggregate demand in the economy (see Chapter 12). It is useful if a small tax change has a significant effect on demand, this however may conflict with the neutrality principle.

7.3 **INCENTIVE/DISINCENTIVE EFFECT** — The extent to which the tax is an incentive or disincentive to work, save, and invest.

7.4 **FLEXIBILITY** and **STABILITY** — The speed with which tax laws can be changed, and those changes implemented.

7.5 **REDISTRIBUTION OF INCOME AND WEALTH** — The effectiveness of the tax system in creating a more equal distribution of income and wealth.

8. Pay As You Earn (PAYE) income tax is an example of a tax which conforms closely to each of the four principles. The tax rates are **PROGRESSIVE** so the higher paid pay a higher tax rate than the lower paid. Tax rates are published and the tax rate made known to the taxpayer. The tax is efficient as the collection of the tax is the responsibility of the employer, who deducts it from incomes and pays it to the Inland Revenue. It is convenient for the taxpayer as it is deducted at source by the employer.

9. **DIRECT TAXES** are borne by those responsible for paying the tax and are levied on either incomes or wealth and are collected by the Inland Revenue. Direct taxes include:

9.1 Income Tax: levied on personal income.

9.2 Corporation Tax: levied on company profits.

9.3 Capital Transfer Tax: chargeable on property with a value above the exemption limit, which passes between persons living or dead.

9.4 Capital Gains Tax: levied on the increase in the value of assets between their acquisition and sale.

10. **INDIRECT TAXES** are taxes on goods and the incidence (burden) of the tax may be passed on through higher prices to the buyer of the goods. The **distribution of the tax incidence is related to the relative elasticities of demand and supply.**

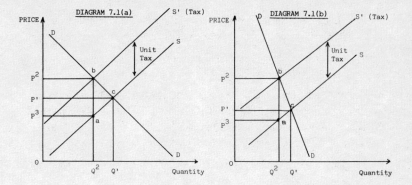

In diagram 7.1(a) a per unit sales tax of a-b shifts the supply curve from S to $S^1$, the vertical distance being the equivalent of the tax. The price to the consumer increases to $P^2$, in this instance the incidence of the tax is borne equally by the producer and the consumer, i.e. the consumer pays $P^1$ — $P^2$ of the tax and the producer pays $P^3$ — $P^1$, because the elasticity of demand and supply are approximately unity. The tax revenue is represented by the rectangle $P^3P^2$ba and the producers revenue is the triangle $0P^3$ $aQ^2$. The triangle abc is referred to as **'deadweight loss'** and is a loss to society as a whole. In diagram 7.1 (b)demand is inelastic and as a result more of the tax burden is passed on to the consumer, here the consumer pays $P^1$ — $P^2$ of the tax and the producer absorbs only $P^3P^1$. (Students should also experiment with different supply elasticities). Indirect taxes include:

10.1   Value Added Tax (VAT): a percentage tax on consumer expenditure.

10.2   Excise duties: are duties levied on domestically produced goods. They are generally **SPECIFIC** taxes in that they are charged in the form of a sum per unit, e.g. petrol duty is levied on each gallon. Other goods subject to excise duties include cigarettes, beer and spirits. These goods are subject to additional taxation because they tend to be in inelastic demand so that the tax does not reduce consumption significantly and the yield of the tax is maintained. Such goods may also bear additional tax because there may be an element of 'paternalism' in that governments may wish to curb excess consumption.

10.3    Customs duties are taxes placed on imported goods. These may be imposed both for revenue purposes and for the protection of domestic industries. (See Chapter 2)

10.4    Motor Vehicles Duties.

10.5    Petroleum Revenue Tax (PRT) levied on the profits from obtaining oil and gas within the U.K. or its territorial sea. This has become an increasingly important source of revenue as a consequence of North Sea Oil discoveries.

10.6    National Insurance contributions.

11.    **REGRESSIVE** taxes are taxes which fall more heavily on the poor than the rich and therefore contravene the equity principle. Indirect taxes are generally held to be regressive. For example, if the duty on a bottle of whisky is £3, for a person earning £30 the tax rate is 10% of income but for a person earning £300 it is only 1% of income. A lump sum tax on income (or **POLL TAX**) is the most regressive form of income tax.

12.    **PROPORTIONATE** taxes are a constant percentage of income, e.g. 10% of income. Corporation tax is an example of a proportionate tax in the U.K. as it is levied on companies as a percentage of profit. If it is accepted that the marginal utility of money declines then proportionate taxation of incomes is inequitable as the sacrifice of 10% of income by a person on a low income is a greater sacrifice than it is to somebody on a high income.

13.    **PROGRESSIVE** taxes are taxes where the tax **RATE** increases, and different 'slices' of income are taxed at different rates. Progressive taxes therefore fall most heavily on the rich and are generally held to be the most equitable method of taxation. It has long been an accepted contention that taxation should be related to **ABILITY TO PAY** on the grounds of **EQUITY** (fairness) between individuals. This inevitably leads to consideration of the **TAX RATE** and two approaches can be identified.

(i)    **EQUALITY OF SACRIFICE:** that the total burden on the nation should be equalized between individuals.

(ii)    **THE BENEFIT PRINCIPLE:** that people should be taxed according to the benefit they receive from the tax system.

45

Progressive taxation of incomes can be justified on the grounds of **EQUALITY OF SACRIFICE,** given the assumption that the **MARGINAL UTILITY OF MONEY DECLINES** e.g. taking £1 in tax from a person earning £100 per week does not involve the same sacrifice of utility as taking £1 from a person earning £1000 per week. The major disadvantage which is claimed for the progressive taxation of incomes is that they operate as a **DISINCENTIVE** to work and effort. Evidence on this is however inconclusive.

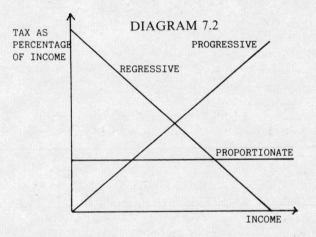

DIAGRAM 7.2

14. When governments fail to cover all their expenditure from taxation they finance the deficit by borrowing. The cumulative total of outstanding debts owed by successive governments is referred to as the **NATIONAL DEBT.** The major part of the debt is in the form of different government securities some of which is long term debt and some short term. Much of the debt is held by institutions such as banks, insurance companies and pension funds, and much of the debt is marketable in that it can be bought and sold on secondary markets such as the stock exchange and the money market. The debt has tended to grow most rapidly during wars when it is impossible for governments to finance all of their expenditure from taxation. Growth of the debt is not in itself a bad thing provided its growth rate is not significantly faster than the rate of growth of Gross Domestic Product.

## SELF ASSESSMENT QUESTIONS

1. State the four principles of taxation.

2. Distinguish between direct and indirect taxation.

3. Distinguish between regressive and progressive taxation.

4. Why is progressive taxation considered to be more equitable than proportionate taxation?

5. What is the National Debt?

## Chapter 8

# THE BANKING SYSTEM & THE CONTROL OF CREDIT

1.  In this chapter we will discuss the structure of the U.K. banking system, the role of the Bank of England, the process by which the commercial banks can create credit and the way in which this credit creating ability is controlled by the Bank of England.

2.  **THE BANK OF ENGLAND** (referred to as 'The Bank') is the institution in the U.K. which is vested with the control of the banking system and, jointly with the Treasury, the implementation of the government's monetary policy. Banks which undertake these responsibilities are referred to as **CENTRAL BANKS** or **RESERVE BANKS** and are found in most industrialised countries.

3.  Since its founding in 1694 the Bank of England has always been closely associated with government policy, a fact which was explicitly recognised when it was taken into public ownership in 1946. The Bank is managed by a board of directors, known as the Court, which consists of a Governor, Deputy Governor and 16 Directors, all appointed by the crown. For accounting purposes the Bank is divided into two functions each producing its own balance sheet.

3.1  **THE ISSUE DEPARTMENT** is responsible for the notes in circulation and their issue.

3.2  **THE BANKING DEPARTMENT** is responsible for the other functions of the Bank of England and the Commercial Banks.

4.  The **BANK CHARTER ACT** of 1844 allowed the note issue to exceed the stock of gold backing the issue. Notes not backed by gold are known as the **FIDUCIARY ISSUE**. Since 1931 when the 'Gold Standard' was abandoned, the whole of the note issue has been Fiduciary. It is no longer backed by gold and neither is it convertible into gold, its backing now being confidence in its value.

5.  The responsibilities of the Bank of England can be summarised as follows:

5.1  It acts as banker to the government, and as such it keeps the accounts of the government departments. In order to ensure that the government always has sufficient finance for its expenditure it manages the government's short term borrowing requirement through the Treasury Bill issue and by making advances. It also manages the longer term debt of the public sector, maintains the stock register, pays dividends, and conducts new issues.

It is also responsible for providing financial advice to the government.

5.2 It is responsible, together with the Treasury, for implementing the government's monetary policy.

5.3 It is the 'bankers' bank'. The commercial banks maintain their balances in current accounts with the Bank. It also provides them with advice and assistance.

5.4 The Bank is the sole authority responsible for issuing notes in England and Wales.

5.5 The Bank acts on behalf of the government on the foreign exchange market when intervention is felt to be necessary to support the pound.

5.6 It acts as 'Lender of Last Resort' to the banking system. If there is a problem of liquidity in the banking system the Bank will give assistance.

5.7 The Bank participates in the activities of such international agencies as the International Monetary Fund and the International Bank for Reconstruction and Development (IBRD).

5.8 The Bank also acts as banker to foreign central banks.

5.9 A most important role is the supervising of the banking and financial institutions in order to ensure their stability and efficient operation. When part of the system is in difficulty the Bank will provide support so as to prevent any undermining of the stability of the system as a whole. The major institutions take advice and leadership from the Bank partly because of its pre-eminent role in the system, but also because in the final analysis it may be essential to their survival.

6. **THE MONEY MARKET** is a general term used for a variety of financial institutions and includes:

6.1 Discount Houses

6.2 Commercial Banks

6.3    Merchant Banks (also known as "Accepting Houses").

6.4    The Foreign Exchange Market.

7.    **THE DISCOUNT MARKET** comprises of the twelve institutions which are members of the London Discount Market Association (LDMA). The original function of Discount Houses was to provide cash immediately, less a discount, to holders of Bills of Exchange which were not due for payment until after three months or longer. The Discount Houses are now recognised as occupying a central role in the financial system. They act in an intermediary role between the Bank of England and the Commercial Banks. The Bank of England utilises the Discount Market to implement its money market operations as part of its overall monetary policy.

7.1    To the Commercial Banks the Discount Market provides a form of investment which has the two desirable characteristics of being both **HIGHLY LIQUID** (i.e. can easily and quickly be repaid), and **SAFE**. Because the Commercial Banks can call in this money at very short notice it is referred to as **MONEY AT CALL**. The Discount Houses use these funds to invest in short-term assets such as Treasury Bills and commercial bills.

7.2.    Should the Discount Houses find themselves short of funds, for example if the banks call in their investments, then the Discount Houses can borrow from the Bank of England against suitable collateral. Because the terms of such lending, such as interest rates and duration of the loan, are so severe, the Bank of England is referred to as the **LENDER OF LAST RESORT**. These stringent conditions are imposed because the arrangement is not intended to be part of the everyday operations of the Bank of England but as a true last resort.

7.3    This last resort borrowing facility is extended only to the Discount Houses. In return for this privilege the Discount Houses are expected to tender (offer to buy) each week the full issue of Treasury Bills on offer. Normally other institutions will also want to buy them so the Discount Houses will only be required to buy a part of the issue, but in the event of there being a deficiency of demand the government can be assured that all the issue will be taken up and can therefore be certain of meeting its short-term borrowing requirement.

7.4 The Bank of England does not deal directly with the Commercial Banks, and the Discount Houses play an intermediary role between them. The Bank of England does not lend directly to the banks but does lend to, or buy bills from, the Discount Houses. In this way the Bank of England increases the stock of balances at the Central Bank which is available to the Commercial Banks. If the Commercial Banks run short of balances they call in their 'money at call' from the Discount Houses. These funds have however been reinvested in various short term assets and in order to meet their commitments the Discount Houses will be forced to utilise the services of the 'lender-of last resort' — the Bank of England. By borrowing from the Bank of England the Discount Houses pass on these Central Bank balances to the Commercial Banks. The Discount Houses could be said to act as a 'buffer' between the Bank of England and the banking system.

8.   The 1979 Banking Act introduced a category of bank referred to as **LICENSED DEPOSIT-TAKERS** (LDT's) and the term 'recognized bank'. To become a recognized bank a certain number of conditions such as minimum capital, range of financial services, and financial standing, had to be met. Institutions offering a narrower range of services and of generally smaller size were licensed to take deposits from the public and were to be known as Licensed Deposit Takers — many of the finance houses are LDT's.

9.   **TREASURY BILLS** are issued each week by the Bank of England on behalf of the government and are one of the means by which the government covers its short term borrowing requirement. The amounts vary between £5,000 and £1 million and are normally issued for a period  of 91 days after which they are redeemable.

10.   **GOVERNMENT STOCKS (GILTS).** The government also raises revenue through the sale of longer dated (or undated) securities. These are sold by the Bank's broker on the securities market,and as they are less liquid than Treasury Bills they tend to be purchased outside the banking sector as well as within it. Government stocks can be bought and sold also on the secondary market (i.e. retraded after being acquired) and as they carry a fixed rate of interest the yield will vary inversely with the price (see Chapter 15).

11.   **COMMERCIAL BANKS** are the vast majority of banks which conduct normal banking business. The term **LONDON CLEARING**

**BANKS (LCB's)** refers to the six banks which between them carry out the largest proportion of the cash distribution and money transmission activities (cheques etc.). The six clearing banks are Barclays, Coutts, Midland, National Westminster, Lloyds and William and Glyn's. The settlement of transfers of indebtedness, which are required as a result of drawings by cheque or other means, is carried out through the Bankers' Clearing House or Bankers' Automated Clearing Services which were set up by the clearing banks themselves for this purpose.

12.    Much inter-bank indebtedness is self cancelling. For example, many of the cheques drawn on Barclays by Lloyds can be offset against cheques drawn on Lloyds by Barclays, so much of this inter-bank indebtedness is self cancelling. This offsetting is carried out by the Clearing House and at the end of the day only the net indebtedness which is left is adjusted through the Commercial Banks' current accounts at the Bank of England.

13.    One of the main functions of the Commercial Banks is to accept the deposits of their customers. Deposits can be held in one of three ways:

13.1    **CURRENT ACCOUNTS (SIGHT DEPOSITS):** These accounts do not earn interest and may be subject to charges for transactions. They are normally held for their convenience as a means of payment by cheque and they can be withdrawn on demand.

13.2    **DEPOSIT ACCOUNTS (TIME DEPOSITS):** These accounts earn interest and cannot be transferred by cheque. For large withdrawals a period of notice may be required, although today most banks show a degree of flexibility over this.

13.3    **LARGE DEPOSITS:** Larger deposits attract a higher rate of interest. For deposits of about £50,000 or more a **CERTIFICATE OF DEPOSIT (CD)** may be issued. These have a maturity of between 3 months and 5 years and as they are **NEGOTIABLE INSTRUMENTS** they can be traded. The banks find them a useful means of raising large sums of money for fixed periods, holder of CD's find them useful as they can be sold if funds are required immediately.

14.    Commercial Banks like all companies need to earn a profit for their shareholders. This requirement however creates a dilemma for banking operations. Banks also have obligations to their depositors

to pay them upon demand and to safeguard their deposits. When a customer makes a deposit with a commercial bank that deposit will be reinvested either in loans or on the money market, or elsewhere; but what is important is that the customer believes his deposit is safe. If customers collectively feared for the safety of their deposits and demanded them all back at the same time the bank would be unable to pay them out and in the absence of assistance from the Central Bank, may collapse. This is referred to as a 'run on the bank' and was common during the recession in the U.S.A. during the late 1920's. In order to be able to pay on demand the banks need to maintain a percentage of their total deposits in the form of cash **(the cash ratio)** and some in the form of assets which are easy to liquidate **("money at call")**. The commercial banks have found that they can operate effectively on a cash ratio of about 8% which is sufficient to meet the everyday demands for cash. The desire to make profit however conflicts with the need to maintain liquidity in a system based almost entirely upon confidence, as the more profitable investments tend to be less liquid. Also profits are higher the more risky the investment, but a high level of risk may result in a loss of confidence. The art of successful banking is therefore to maintain a balanced 'portfolio'of

| The Sterling Assets of The London Clearing Banks (May 1983) | £mn | Per Cent |
|---|---|---|
| Notes and Coin | 857 | .13 |
| Balances with the Bank of England | 321 | .48 |
| Treasury Bills | 279 | .42 |
| Other Bills | 1,226 | 1.90 |
| Money at Call with the London Discount Market | 2,885 | 4.30 |
| Other Market Loans | 8,754 | 13.10 |
| Advances | 47,358 | 70.70 |
| British Government Stocks | 2,643 | 3.94 |
| Other Investments | 2,696 | 4.03 |
| | 67,019 | |

SOURCE: Bank of England Quarterly Bulletin

TABLE 8.1

investments. Bank investments therefore contain a range of investments from very low to modest risk, and with varying degrees of liquidity. Table 8.1 lists the assets held by the London Clearing Banks (May, 1983). Prior to 1971 the banks were required to maintain 28% of their assets in investments which were highly liquid, this was referred to as the 'liquidity ratio', and an 8% cash ratio; both of which were abandoned in 1971. For operating purposes however banks still require a cash ratio and some of their assets in investments which are easy to liquidate. Because of the large proportion of transactions which are now carried out by cheque the banks tend to maintain a smaller cash ratio, as can be seen from Table 8.1.

15.   Banks have a powerful ability to **CREATE CREDIT**, and as credit can be considered as a form of money in that it facilitates the purchase of goods, governments need to exert some degree of control over this credit creating ability.

16.   This ability to create credit arises from the fact stated above, that the banks only require a small fraction of their total deposits in the form of cash; just sufficient to meet the daily demands of their customers. This cash ratio is generally a percentage of total deposits and for purposes of illustration we will assume it is 10% (although in reality it could be much smaller). With a cash ratio of 10% a deposit of £50 would be used as the basis for creating £450 in credit money (i.e. £50 is 10% of £500 and £450 + £50 = £500). This is made possible by the fact that when a bank makes an advance to a customer the customer's account is credited and he will then probably use a cheque to obtain the goods he requires, the recipient of the cheque will then redeposit the cheque into the banking system, which because of the operation of the Clearing System has a similar effect to that of redepositing the cheque with the same bank. In diagram 8.1, A has deposited £50 with his bank. With a cash ratio of 10% the bank creates credit for C by crediting his account with £450. C uses this to buy goods for £200 from D and £250 from E, paying them both by cheque. These cheques are eventually redeposited with the bank, and even if.E and D draw some cash, statistically it will be unlikely to be of such an amount that it could not be met from the £50 initial deposit and still leave sufficient for the average cash demand of A. As stated earlier it does not matter if the cheques are deposited with a different bank because of the clearing arrangements, and as they do not draw cash against each other they operate in a similar manner to a single bank.

## DIAGRAM 8.1

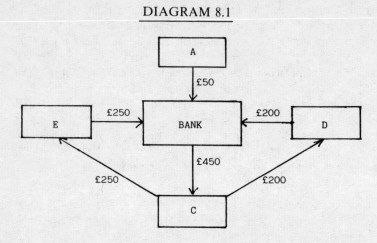

17. This process of credit creation is referred to as the **BANK CREDIT MULTIPLIER**. In order to explain this process further it is necessary to appreciate that a cardinal rule of banking is that they must maintain an **EQUALITY BETWEEN THEIR ASSETS AND LIABILITIES** on their balance sheets. It should also be noted that as far as a bank is concerned **DEPOSITS** appear as a **LIABILITY** on the balance sheets as they have a liability to repay the customer, and **ADVANCES** (loans) appear as **ASSETS**.

18. In order to simplify the explanation of the process of credit creation we will assume initially that the economy's banking system consists of a single bank only. Because of this all credit, also referred to as **CREATED DEPOSITS**, will be deposited with the same bank. If we also assume a 10% cash ratio for ease of calculation we can illustrate the process in table 8.2.

## TABLE 8.2

|  | LIABILITIES (£) |  | ASSETS (£) |  |
|---|---|---|---|---|
| PERIOD 1 | Initial Deposits | 25,000 | Notes and Coin | 25,000 |
| PERIOD 2 | Initial Deposits | 25,000 | Notes and Coin | 25,000 |
|  | Created Deposits | 225,000 | Loans (Credit) | 225,000 |
|  |  | 250,000 |  | 250,000 |

In period 1 the bank has attracted initial deposits from its customers of £25,000. Operating on a cash ratio of 10%, which is considered to be sufficient to meet the average withdrawal, then loans can be advanced to the extent of £225,000 (9 × 25,000). These loans will eventually be spent, probably by cheque, and as we have assumed a single bank they will be redeposited with the same bank, and in period 2 they then show on the liabilities side of the balance sheet in the form of **CREATED DEPOSITS**. It should be noted that initial deposits of £25,000 have served to create credit nine times greater (£225,000). This **MULTIPLE EXPANSION OF CREDIT** is also referred to as the **BANK CREDIT MULTIPLIER**.

19.    Dropping the assumption of a single bank economy makes little difference to the ability to create credit. In a multi-bank system such as the U.K. the only difference is that the initial cash deposits are divided between the various banks, but assuming the same cash ratio is maintained the same **TOTAL** amount of credit will be created. Even if the different banks were not equally successful in attracting deposits only the final distribution will be affected and not the total amount of credit. As mentioned above, although we have a multi-bank system it operates in a similar manner to a single bank system through the operation of the clearing system.

20.   The ability of the banks to create credit is powerful, but not unlimited. Limitations to credit creation are as follows:

20.1   An over extension of credit would **increase the proportion of bad debts** which would undermine both profitability and confidence.

20.2   **The need to maintain liquidity** in a system where confidence is paramount.

20.3   **Controls exerted over the banks by the Bank of England** as part of the government's monetary policy (see Chapter 11).

21.   The principle of sound banking can be summarised as:

21.1   The **balancing of profit and risk** so as to maintain confidence and at the same time produce an adequate return.

21.2   Maintain confidence by demonstrating both **integrity and soundness**.

21.3   To maintain **adequate liquid assets** in order to ensure that withdrawals can be met.

21.4   To ensure that **assets are equal to liabilities** on the balance sheet.


## SELF ASSESSMENT QUESTIONS

1.   What are the main functions of the Bank of England?

2.   What role does the Discount market play in the financial structure?

3.   Describe the function of the Bankers' Clearing House.

4.   Outline the process by which banks can bring about the multiple expansion of credit.

5.   What are the principles of sound banking?

# Chapter 9
# INFLATION

1.  Inflation refers to a **GENERALISED AND SUSTAINED RISE IN THE PRICE LEVEL,** or a **FALL IN THE VALUE OF MONEY,** both of which amount to the same thing — that a unit of currency will buy fewer goods. Inflation does **NOT** refer to the fact that **SOME** goods have become more expensive than others because **RELATIVE PRICES** change constantly according to demand and supply. Inflation refers to the fact that the price of **ALL** goods is rising.

2.  It is not merely the fact that prices are rising which is important but rather the **RATE OF INCREASE.** This is usually stated as the **ANNUAL RATE OF INFLATION** as measured by a **PRICE INDEX,** the most frequently quoted index of inflation is the **RETAIL PRICE INDEX.** There are also manufacturing and wholesale price indices but the Retail Price Index measures inflation as it affects the majority of people. The index is constructed from price data gathered in the **FAMILY EXPENDITURE SURVEY** and is constructed from the prices of a collection of goods and services which enter a typical shopping 'basket', each item being weighted in accordance with its importance in the household budget. The 'basket of goods' is then revalued in each subsequent year at current prices, and inflation is represented by the increase in the index. The composition of the basket is changed periodically to keep abreast of changes in expenditure patterns. The index becomes outdated in its coverage eventually as the year upon which it was based becomes more distant in time. A further weakness is that during periods of rapid inflation the index may exaggerate inflation as consumers substitute those goods which are rising less rapidly in price and therefore become relatively cheaper. Index numbers represent percentage changes rather than absolute changes. For example in the base year the index will be 100; if in the following year the index is 120 then the index has risen by 20 percentage points. (See Appendix 1).

3.  When comparing economic statistics over time it is necessary to **DEFLATE** the data in order to eliminate the effect of inflation. For example, if incomes rise by 20% over a year but prices have risen by 15% the **REAL** increase in incomes is only 5% i.e.

3.1 **MONEY** (or **NOMINAL**) Incomes (or Wages) refers to income in terms of the number of pounds earned.

3.2 **REAL** Incomes (or Wages) refers to the actual increase in purchasing power after allowing for the effects of inflation.

$$\frac{\textbf{MONEY INCOME}}{\textbf{RPI}} \times 100 = \textbf{Real Income}$$

Increases in income may appear far more modest after allowing for the effects of inflation.

4.    It is also necessary to deflate the data when comparing GDP over different time periods in order to estimate the rate of growth of the economy. This is achieved in a similar manner to above by the use of the **IMPLIED DEFLATOR** for GDP. This is obtained by dividing the value of GDP at current prices by GDP at constant (1975) prices.

$$\frac{\textbf{GDP (Nominal)}}{\textbf{GDP (1975 Prices)}} = \textbf{GDP at Constant Prices}$$

5.    Slow rates of inflation of 2-3% will aways be present in a growing economy and may even be conducive to growth itself. When inflation rises to very high levels however the effects can be very damaging on the economy and is therefore unacceptable to most governments. Sustained high rates of inflation, known as **HYPERINFLATION**, have occured several times in history, in particular the German

DIAGRAM 9.1

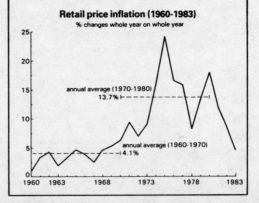

Retail price inflation (1960-1983)
% changes whole year on whole year

annual average (1970-1980) 13.7%

annual average (1960-1970) 4.1%

SOURCE: ECONOMIC PROGRESS REPORT No. 165

inflation of 1923 and the Hungarian inflation of 1944. In Britain the 1970's saw higher rates of inflation than any other period in the twentieth century. Retail prices rose on average by 12.7% per annum between 1970 and 1979, compared with 3.3% between 1953 and 1969, and 2% in 1934-39. Inflation in Britain reached a peak of 24% in 1975 before declining to around 5% in 1984. Diagram 9.1. illustrates the recent trends in inflation.

Although high rates of inflation are considered to be undesirable and most governments give priority to controlling it there are examples of countries enduring very high rates of inflation over sustained periods, in particular South American countries such as Chile and Brazil, but often only at the cost of foregoing democratic freedoms, and abject poverty for a large section of the population.

6.  The **CAUSES** of inflation are the subject of much controversy and academic debate, some of which will be discussed later; it is however common practice to classify inflation into two categories:

### 6.1  DEMAND — PULL INFLATION:

Demand-pull inflation is defined as a situation where **AGGREGATE DEMAND EXCEEDS AGGREGATE SUPPLY AT CURRENT PRICES**, hence prices are 'pulled up' by the total demand for goods and services exceeding what the economy is capable of producing. Inflation of this type is associated with the full employment of resources, where there is spare capacity of either, or, both labour and capital an increase in demand may be achieved without a significant rise in the price level. If resources are fully utilised however it will not be possible in the short run to meet any increase in demand by increasing output and the excess demand can only result in an increase in the price level. An example of Demand-Pull inflation occured during the Korean War (1950/51) when the Western world was unwilling to forego its current consumption of goods following the austerity years after World War II but the Western governments were engaged in a conflict in Korea which was demanding a high level of resource consumption. World demand for resources exceeded what could be supplied and prices rose substantially. Attempting to achieve high rates of economic growth during a period of full employment may also result in excess demand and rising prices.

### 6.2  COST — PUSH INFLATION:

Cost-push inflation is a consequence of rising costs which tend to push up prices. It is **NOT** a consequence of excess demand for goods resulting in increased demand for factors, higher factor prices and therefore higher prices to the consumer. Cost-push inflation occurs when costs rise independently of an increase in demand. Cost inflation can result from some, or all, of the following:

(i) Increases in wages which are greater than the increase in productivity.

(ii) A fall in the exchange rate which increases the cost of imported materials.

(iii) A rise in the cost of imported materials due to other factors abroad, for example the formation of the OPEC cartel and its effect on oil prices in the 1970's.

(iv) Increases in indirect taxation (i.e. taxes on goods and services such as VAT).

Entrepreneurs tend to have a fairly fixed idea of the sort of profit margins they should be making, and as the costs of production rise they attempt to maintain these margins by marking up prices to the consumer.

7. **EXPECTATIONS** play an important role in the inflationary process. As inflation is experienced over a period of time employees tend to start thinking in terms of real wages rather than nominal (money) wages, i.e. they see through the "veil of money", and begin to anticipate inflation. As a result union negotiators start to build a 'hedge' against inflation into wage negotiations. So, for example, if the union wants to gain a 10% increase in real wages for its members and anticipated inflation is 15%, and assuming 5% will be given away during the bargaining process, the union will bargain initially for a 30% increase:

    30%
— 5%   Lost during negotiation
— 15%  Lost due to inflation

    10%   Increase in real wages

If entrepreneurs also anticipate this process and build a similar hedge into their prices and forward contracts then the anticipated inflation will be in the form of a 'self fulfilling prophecy'.

8. If we consider the causes of demand-pull and cost-push inflation we can see quite easily why they may result in a rise in the price level.

61

They do not explain however how they can generate a sustained and generalised rise in the price level over a period of time, rather than a once-and-for-all increase. If however, we combine them with the effects of the expectations described above, and extend the effects to include the exchange rate and overseas trade we can see how a rise in the price level can start a **WAGE/PRICE SPIRAL**, resulting in a sustained period of inflation. Such a process is outlined in Diagram 9.1, and it should be noted that in the example the process begins with a period of demand-pull inflation which becomes transformed into cost-push inflation, but the process could start just as easily with cost-push inflation.

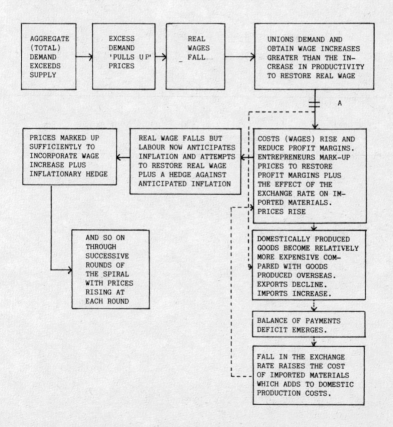

DIAGRAM 9.1   THE WAGE PRICE SPIRAL

9.   Keynesians (after J.M. Keynes, see Chapter 12) see costs as being the main determinants of prices and the most important element in costs is considered to be wages. They therefore suggest that the best way to control inflation is to control wages. Wage controls, such as the various **INCOMES POLICIES** which were pursued in the 1960's and 1970's, should therefore be imposed at point A in Diagram 9.1 to keep the wage increases at or below the rate of increase of productivity. Such policies can be either:

   (i)   Voluntary
   (ii)  Statutory

The results of such policies are however inconclusive and their effects on inflation appear to be only temporary.

10.   **MONETARISTS** consider that inflation is due solely to the over expansion of the money supply by governments and that attempts to control inflation by any means other than the strict control of the money supply will be doomed to failure (see Chapter 16 for further details).

11.   **THE QUANTITY THEORY OF MONEY** attempts to explain the relationship between the supply of money and the price level. In its most basic form it can be expressed as

**MV = PT**

*where*
M   = the money supply, or stock
V   = the velocity of circulation of money
P   = the price level
T   = the volume of transactions

The left hand side of the equation represents the total amount of money used to finance transactions in a given period and the right hand side total expenditures in that period. Both sides are therefore equal. Because velocity (V) is measured as PT/M the equation is sometimes referred to as a tautology (self evident). It is still useful however in identifying the variables which influence the value of money. Classical economic theory assumed that both V and T would be constant in the short run. Any change in the money supply (M) would therefore have an equal effect on the price level (P).

i.e.                          $$M\overline{V} = P\overline{T}$$

If there were a substantial reserve of unemployed resources however an increase in M, with V remaining constant would result in increased output and therefore transactions, with P remaining unchanged.

There is much controversy however over whether or not V is in fact constant. If V varies then it is quite conceivable that an increase in M could be offset by a reduction in V leaving the price level (P) unchanged. During deep recessions such as the 1930's, spending was greatly reduced, which did in fact result in a reduction in V. During periods of hyper-inflation one of the characteristics is a rapid increase in V as people spend their cash balances as quickly as possible before they lose their value. More recent adaptations of the Quantity Theory will be discussed in the chapter on Monetarism (Chapter 16).

12.   In an open economy such as Britain's it is not possible to isolate the domestic inflation rate from inflation in the rest of the world and inflation can be transmitted through the relative exchange rates. It will be recalled from Chapter 4 that in the long run **PURCHASING POWER PARITY** theory undoubtedly holds true although there may be deviations from it in the short run. There is therefore a transmission mechanism through which inflation can become

internationally transmitted. It should be noted in this context that the high rate of inflation of the 1970's was by no means restricted to Britain but also appeared in most industrialised countries.

13. Inflation is generally considered to be undesirable for the following reasons:

13.1 The longer debtors can delay repayment of debts the less they repay in real terms, therefore debtors gain and creditors lose and eventually there is a reluctance to give credit. As credit is the basis of trade, inflation eventually results in a breakdown of trading relationships.

13.2 The reluctance to give credit results in higher interest rates.

13.3 There is an arbitrary income redistribution between groups in society. Those on fixed incomes, non union labour, and weaker groups generally lose out to well organised, stronger groups or those who set their own incomes through commission or profits.

13.4 The value of savings is rapidly eroded leaving the saving classes embittered.

14. The dangers from inflation are by no means all economic and possibly the greatest problems of inflation arise from the social and political strains it places upon society, in particular its divisiveness between different groups within society. For these reasons most democratic governments give high priority in their economic policies to curbing it.

## SELF ASSESSMENT QUESTIONS

1. Distinguish between Cost-Push and Demand-Pull inflation.

2. Outline what is meant by a 'wage price spiral'.

3. State the Quantity Theory of Money and outline how it relates the money supply to the price level.

4. How is inflation measured?

5. Explain the role of expectations in generating wage inflation.

# APPENDIX

## The Construction of a Retail Price Index

```
            YEAR 1 (Y₁)                    |              YEAR 2 (Y₂)
                                           |          INDEX
                     BASE    WEIGHTED      |          Y2 as    WEIGHTED
                     YEAR    PRICE         |          a %      PRICE
Item     WEIGHTS  PRICE INDEX   INDEX      |  PRICE   of Y1    INDEX

Potatoes    5      10p    100     500      |  15p      150      750

Milk        3      30p    100     300      |  39p      130      390

Meat        2     £1.50   100     200      |  £1.65    110      220
                                ──────     |                  ──────
                          10    1000       |          10      1360

              BASE YEAR INDEX  = 100       |   YEAR 2 INDEX  =   136


                      YEAR 1  =  100
                      YEAR 2  =  136

     An increase in the Retail Price Index of 36 percentage points.
```

## STAGES

1. Select appropriate weights reflecting the importance of the item in the household budget.

2. Set Base Year Index = 100. Weights × Index = Weighted Price Index. The sum of the Weighted Price Index ÷ the sum of the Weights = Base Year Index.

3. Second Year Index calculated as Year 2 prices as a percentage of Year 1 prices.

4. Year 2 Weighted Price Index = $Y_2$ Index × Weight.

5. Year 2 Index = the sum of the Weighted Price Index ÷ the sum of the Weights.

6. The procedure is continued in a similar manner for each subsequent year.

# Chapter 10

## DEFINING THE MONEY SUPPLY

1.  Before we consider the policy instruments which may be utilised by government in the control of the money supply we need to define precisely what we mean by the money supply. (Much of this chapter is quite technical and for A level students who are new to the subject it will suffice if they learn the definitions of M0, M1 and £M3 as summarised in diagram 10.1). It is suggested that students read the section on money in the companion volume to this text (Concepts in Micro Economics).

2.  Money can be defined as anything which is generally acceptable in return for goods and services, however in an advanced economy such a definition is not sufficiently precise for operational purposes. The main definitions used in the U.K. are M1 and £M3. M1 is generally referred to as a 'narrow' definition of money and £M3 as a 'broad' definition. The components of these definitions are as follows:

> M1 = Notes and coin in circulation with the public + sterling current account deposits held by the private sector with the banks.

> M3 = Notes and coins in circulation + current and deposit accounts in sterling and non sterling of both the private and public sectors.

> Sterling (£) M3 = Notes and coin in circulation + U.K. private sector current and deposit accounts + U.K. public sector sterling deposits.

The difference between M3 and £M3 is the inclusion in M3 of residents' holdings of non sterling (foreign currency) deposits. More emphasis has been given in recent years to the Sterling £M3 definition.

Although M1 and £M3 have been the most widely used definitions over recent years, there have been a number of new definitions which should be noted.

Because certain other forms of liquid asset can be converted into means of payment with little delay the Bank of England introduced in 1980 two definitions which include holdings of liquid assets other than cash and bank deposits. These definitions refer to Private Sector Liquidity (PSL) and are summarised as:

PSL1 = Notes and Coin + Private Sector deposit accounts + Other money market instruments and certificates of tax deposits held by the private sector.

PSL2 = PSL1 + Deposits with building societies and the National Savings Bank and National Savings securities.

These 'broad' monetary aggregates have been supplemented with two further recent 'narrow' definitions, M2 and M0:

M2 = Notes and coin + U.K. private sector (non interest bearing) current accounts in U.K. banks + interest bearing deposits held by the private sector in U.K. banks and building societies for transactions purposes.

M0 = Notes and coin + banks' holding of cash (till money) plus banks' operational balances at the Bank of England (bankers' balances).

3. It would appear that the introduction of M0 in March 1984 was a consequence of the difficulty in achieving targets for monetary growth utilising broader definitions such as M3. Broad measures give an indication of the growth of liquidity in the economy whilst narrower definitions give a better idea of how money is being used for transactions as opposed to saving.

4. The definitions above are often referred to as monetary 'aggregates' as they aggregate together various forms of 'money'.

4.1 **NARROW MONEY** refers generally to money held predominantly for spending immediately or in the near future on goods and services, i.e. for transactions purposes.

4.2 **BROAD MONEY** refers generally to money held for transactions purposes **and** as a store of value. When we say that it provides a guide to liquidity, we mean that it provides an indicator of the private sectors' holding of relatively liquid assets — i.e. assets which **could** be converted with relative ease into spending on goods and services without capital loss.

5. Narrow and broad definitions can be summarised as:

**NARROW** = M0, M1 and M2
**BROAD** = M3, £M3, PSL1, PSL2.

Students should note that probably the most important to concentrate upon are: M0, M1 and £M3, which are summarised in Diagram 10.1.

DIAGRAM 10.1

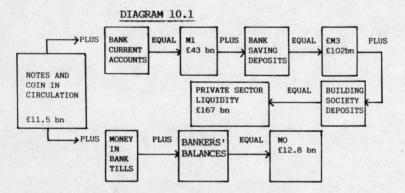

6. **DOMESTIC CREDIT EXPANSION (DCE)** measures the increase in the money stock (£M3) plus any deficit (or less any surplus) on the balance of payments. A balance of payments deficit reducing the money stock and a surplus increasing it. DCE is therefore a measure of the increase in the money stock caused by domestically generated credit and excludes the monetary effects of the balance of payments.

7. **THE PUBLIC SECTOR BORROWING REQUIREMENT (PSBR)** refers to the deficit between the income and expenditure of the public sector (in particular central and local government). It arises because governments generally fail to balance their budgets (see Chapter 12) i.e. their expenditures are greater than their incomes from taxation and other sources. This deficit is usually financed by debt sales (government bonds etc.) to the 'non bank' private sector, borrowing from the banking system, borrowing from overseas, or by issuing more cash (notes and coin) to the public. There is a close relationship between the PSBR and the money supply, which will be explored more closely in Chapter 16.

8. If we consider, for the purposes of our discussion, control of the money supply to refer to the Sterling M3 definition, we can define the **GROWTH** of £M3 as:

$\Delta£M3$ = The increase in bank lending to the private sector **PLUS** the public sector borrowing requirement **MINUS** sales of public sector debt to non-banks.

From this definition we can identify those variables for which policies will be required in the control of the money supply:

8.1 Bank lending to the private sector (Credit Policy).

8.2 The control of the size of the PSBR.

8.3 The sale of more public sector debt to the non banks (debt management policy).

9

DIAGRAM 10.2

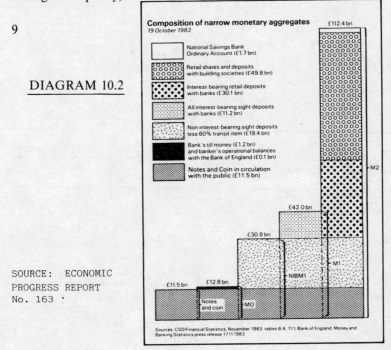

SOURCE: ECONOMIC
PROGRESS REPORT
No. 163 :

**SELF ASSESSMENT QUESTIONS**

1. Distinguish between 'broad' and 'narrow' definitions of money.

2. Define M0, M1 amd £M3.

3. What is meant by Domestic Credit Expansion (DCE)?

4. What are the components of an increase in Sterling M3?

# Chapter 11
# INSTRUMENTS OF MONETARY POLICY

1. From our previous discussion it is evident that one of the main components of the money supply is credit money. If the government is to control the money supply it is therefore essential that it has some means of controlling the ability of the commercial banks to create credit.

2. In the period prior to 1971 credit creation was controlled in two ways:

2.1DIRECT CONTROLS. Direct controls were either of the QUANTITATIVE type or the QUALITATIVE type.

(a) QUANTITATIVE CONTROLS took the form of CEILINGS on the amount of credit which the main banks could create, and on Hire Purchase terms.

(b) QUALITATIVE CONTROLS were instructions regarding the composition of bank lending, i.e. those sectors of the economy to which the banks could lend, for example, preference to finance for exporters, or finance to be used for investment purposes.

2.2 The other main instrument of control during this period was that the banks had to observe a 28% liquidity ratio i.e. they had to hold a stock of specified liquid assets equal to 28% of their deposits, plus an 8% cash ratio.

The main emphasis during this period was on direct controls.

3. In 1971 a new system of controls over credit creation was introduced, known as COMPETITION AND CREDIT CONTROL. These measures were intended to encourage greater competition in the monetary system and at the same time rely more heavily on market forces as a method of control, rather than direct controls. The new system of controls emphasised short term interest rates and the composition of the banks' balance sheets. The new regulations introduced a 12½% RESERVE ASSET RATIO whereby all banks were to hold certain specified assets whose value was not to fall below 12½% of their ELIGIBLE LIABILITIES. The RESERVE ASSETS included:

(i) Balances with the Bank of England (other than Special Deposits).
(ii) Treasury Bills.
(iii) Money at call with the London Discount Market.
(iv) Gilt edged stock with less than a year to run to maturity.
(v) Local Authority and Commercial Bills eligible for rediscount at the Bank of England.

Most of these assets originate in the public sector and are therefore under the control of the Bank of England, and any reduction in their availability would mean that the banks would be forced to reduce the level of their deposits in order to maintain the $12\frac{1}{2}\%$ ratio, and this would therefore restrict their ability to create credit. Some commentators suggest that the purpose of the $12\frac{1}{2}\%$ ratio was primarily intended to ensure that banks continued to invest on the traditional money markets and that the fractional reserve aspect was intended to be of secondary importance, but this secondary role became increasingly prominent. These regulations were abandoned in August 1981 (see later).

4. **SPECIAL DEPOSITS** constituted a further instrument of control. These were first introduced in 1960 but became more important after the introduction of C.C.C. Special deposits are called in from the banks by the Bank of England and are held in a special account. While they are held by the Bank of England they do not form part of the banks' current assets (They are in fact 'frozen'). As these balances cannot be drawn upon like the commercial banks' normal Bank of England balances, they cannot be included as reserve assets. Special Deposits therefore reduce the liquidity of the banks and in so doing restrict their ability to create credit.

5. By 1973 it became apparent that the level of interest rates was not in itself sufficient to control the growth of the money stock and in December 1973 an element of direct control was reintroduced in the form of the **SUPPLEMENTARY SPECIAL DEPOSITS SCHEME**, known generally as 'the **CORSET**'. Under the scheme the Bank of England set a target rate of growth for each bank's interest bearing deposits. If the actual rate of growth of deposits exceeded the target rate a deposit had to be made in an account with the Bank of England. These deposits received no interest and grew progressively larger the more the banks exceeded the target growth rate for

deposits. The effect of this 'corset' was similar to that of the ceilings imposed before 1971. The corset was however by-passed as credit was diverted into uncontrolled channels, a process referred to as "disintermediation"; and also by the raising of funds through the issue of commercial bills — known as the "bill leak". The failure of the corset resulted in its abandonment in 1980, ordinary special deposits were however retained.

6. **OPEN MARKET OPERATIONS** are the means by which the Bank of England influences the stock of financial assets and thereby indirectly the lending of the banks. If the Bank of England's broker sells government securities on the market purchasers of these securities pay by cheques drawn on their banks in favour of the Bank of England. When these cheques are presented for payment the banks' deposits are reduced at the Bank of England. This reduces the liquid assets of the banks and to restore the ratio of assets to liabilities the banks are forced to reduce the amount of lending. When the Bank of England enters the market to purchase securities and pays for them with cheques drawn on itself it has the opposite effect as these cheques will be deposited in the sellers' bank accounts increasing the commercial banks' asset base and enabling them to create additional credit. To summarise:

6.1   The **SALE** of bonds **REDUCES** the money supply.

6.2   The **PURCHASE** of bonds **INCREASES** the money supply.

7.   Creating a reduction in liquidity by the use of open market operations also allowed the Bank of England to pursue its **INTEREST RATE POLICY**. In order to restore liquidity the banks would be forced to 'call in' money from the discount market (see Chapter 4). As the discount market would have this money invested in Treasury Bills, Bills of Exchange and Commercial Loans, it may have to turn to the "lender of the last resort" — the Bank of England. The rate at which the Bank of England was prepared to lend to the discount market was known as **MINIMUM LENDING RATE (MLR)**. An increase in MLR would reduce the profitability of the discount houses' operations and they would be forced to adjust their interest rates to restore their profitability, and all other interest rates, on bank loans, mortgages, hire purchase etc. would follow suit. In 1981 however the Bank of England ceased declaring an official MLR, but may still intervene to influence short-term interest rates. MLR was used again in January 1985 when the government announced a

2% increase in MLR in order to bring about a general rise in interest rates in support of the pound which was coming under intense pressure from the dollar on the foreign exchange markets.

8. **FUNDING** operations refer to the practice of managing the government's debt in order to influence the money supply. These operations involve the replacing of maturing debts with longer-term securities in order to reduce the amount of liquidity in the economy, or vice versa to increase liquidity. A secondary consequence of such activities is however to influence bond prices and therefore interest rates.

9. Competition and Credit Control and its main provision the $12\frac{1}{2}\%$ Reserve Asset Ratio, was abandoned in August 1981 and was replaced by a system of **MONETARY BASE CONTROL** which was intended to give the government tighter control over the monetary aggregates (M1 and M3).

10. **MONETARY BASE CONTROL** is a system which attempts to control the growth of the money stock by the Central Bank controlling the growth of the monetary base. The monetary base is the commercial banks' deposits with the Bank of England. As mentioned above, the bank can affect the size of these deposits by buying or selling securities on the open market. If the authorities set a target for the growth of the monetary base which was intended to restrict the amount of bank lending and the banks exceed the lending target they would run short of base money, assuming a stable ratio between holdings of base money and deposits, the banks would be forced to obtain base money to restore the ratio. In order to obtain the required base money they would be forced to bid for it on the money market which would force up interest rates. The interest rates charged to borrowers would then have to be raised to restore profitability and the demand for credit would be reduced, thereby eliminating the excess growth in the money supply. The implication of this method of control is a degree of loss of control over interest rates and possibly considerable short run fluctuations. The main provisions introduced in August 1981 were as follows:

10.1 All institutions in the monetary sector with eligible liabilities of over £10 million were required to hold $\frac{1}{2}\%$ of their eligible liabilities in non-interest-bearing balances at the Bank of England.

10.2   Eligible banks were required to hold an average of 6%, but never less than 4%, on a daily basis, of their eligible liabilities in secured money with the discount houses. This was to ensure that the traditional channels for such funds continued to be used.

10.3   MLR was suspended. Money market operations were to be conducted with reference to a narrow band for short-term interest rates. (MLR was next used in January 1975 — see 11.7).

11.   Since 1976 governments have followed the policy of announcing **TARGETS** for the growth of the money stock, from 1976 to 1981 for M3 only, but in 1982 also for M1 and PSL2. In March 1984 the Treasury announced that monetary targets would be set for five years ahead rather than three as previously and would include a target for M0. Problems have been encountered in the past in achieving targets due to the difficulty of estimating the demand for bank lending, the fact that other objectives were sometimes given priority over control of the money stock, and other factors which resulted in an increase in the stock of money, for example one of the main elements in the creation of money is the Public Sector Borrowing Requirement — which is not under the direct control of the Bank of England.

12.   Methods of monetary control have tended to reflect the prevailing attitude towards the importance of the role of money in the economy. In the era of the 1950's and 1960's following the Radcliffe Report money was not perceived as being a particularly important instrument of policy, but as this perception changed during the 1960's the money supply was seen as being increasingly important, a development which was reflected to a limited extent in the changes introduced in Competition and Credit Control 1971. Throughout the 1970's, with the growing acceptance of the ideas of the 'monetarist' school of thought, money was viewed with growing importance, and came to be seen by many as being the most important of economic variables; culminating in the system of Monetary Base Control introduced in 1981.


**SELF ASSESSMENT QUESTIONS**

1.   Distinguish between qualitative and quantitative controls over bank lending.

2. What are Special Deposits?

3. What was the 12½% Reserve Asset Ratio introduced in the 1971 Competition and Credit Control regulations?

4. How does the Bank of England utilise Open Market Operations in order to influence the money supply?

5. How does the system of Monetary Base Control introduced in 1981 operate?

# Chapter 12
## DEMAND MANAGEMENT —
## THE KEYNESIAN MODEL

1.  The idea that governments should attempt to manage the economy in order to achieve full employment owes much to J.M. (Lord) Keynes. His book The General Theory of Employment, Interest and Money (1936) (referred to as The General Theory) was probably the most influential work on economics of the twentieth century and was used as the basis for managing the economies of the Western world for the thirty years following 1945. This text attempts to do no more than explain in simple terms some of the ideas involved in the Keynesian Model of demand management and it is recommended that you supplement it at a later stage with reading from a more advanced text.

2.  In order to understand Keynes's contribution it is useful to very briefly outline how economists before Keynes, referred to loosely as the 'Classical economists', viewed the working of the economy. This is not an attempt to analyse the ideas of any particular economist but merely an overview of how the economy was considered to operate. Classical economists believed that two essential principles prevailed:

    (i)   That the Quantity Theory of Money operated (see Chapter 9).

    (ii)   That Say's Law of Markets applied.

Say's Law of Markets is usually expressed as 'supply creates its own demand', or more literally that 'production creates the market for goods'. If these two principles are accepted it implies that the following points also apply:

    (iii)   Prices and wages are flexible.

    (iv)   Savings and investment are always brought into balance by movements in the interest rate, and all savings are therefore reinvested.

If we accept these principles then over-production of goods and unemployment become impossible, the economy will always tend towards equilibrium and by definition **EQUILIBRIUM IN THE ECONOMY COINCIDED WITH FULL EMPLOYMENT.**

3.   If we consider the process by which equilibrium was considered to be established, in very simple terms, we can see that prolonged periods of **INVOLUNTARY** unemployment were not possible. In a situation were high unemployment did exist competition for jobs would depress wage rates until they became so low that entrepreneurs would take on additional labour. The very act of producing the extra output would, according to Say's Law, generate sufficient purchasing power in the economy for its consumption. Also, according to the Quantity Theory, money balances were held only for making transactions.

It was not possible therefore for a situation of deficient total demand to exist. Savings could not exceed investment except in the short-run because the rate of interest would fall deterring some saving whilst encouraging investment until they came into equilibrium, and vice versa if attempted investment exceeded savings.

4.   The essential point was that in the absence of government intervention the economy would always tend back to the **FULL EMPLOYMENT EQUILIBRIUM**. Any unemployment which then existed was **VOLUNTARY** and occured because workers were not willing to work for low enough wages.

5.   The experience of the prolonged depression of the 1920's and 1930's and the failure of the economy to move automatically back to a situation of full employment caused Keynes to question the fundamental principles of the Classical Economists. Keynes argued that there was no longer an automatic tendency for the economy to move back to full employment because of changes which have taken place in the structure of the economy which made invalid some of the classical assumptions. In particular:

   (i)   Wages were no longer flexible in a downwards direction due to the growth of Trade Unions.

   (ii)   The direct Quantity Theory relationship between money and prices was no longer valid.

   (iii)   Saving and investment are carried out by distinctly different groups and there is no reason why what firms are **PLANNING** to invest is necessarily the same   as what they are **ACTUALLY** able to invest. Also, what individuals are planning to save is not necessarily the same as what they actually manage to save. An increased desire to save by the whole community actually reduces consumption, and therefore incomes, resulting in **LESS** actual saving (known as the **PARADOX OF THRIFT**). It was possible therefore for **PLANNED INVESTMENT AND SAVINGS TO DIFFER, AND THAT EQUALITY BETWEEN SAVINGS AND INVESTMENT IS BROUGHT ABOUT NOT BY CHANGES IN THE INTEREST RATE BUT FLUCTUATIONS IN INCOME AND THEREFORE EMPLOYMENT.** As there was no tendency for the situation to change during the 1920's and 1930's the economy could be assumed to be in equilibrium **BUT WITH A HIGH LEVEL OF UNEMPLOYMENT.** What Keynes argued was that a modern economy could be in equilibrium with **ANY** level of unemployment and stay there indefinitely. It was in fact **DEMAND** which was deficient and the only way to achieve full employment was for the government to intervene and raise the level of demand thereby shifting the equilibrium point of the economy to coincide with the full employment level. **KEYNES'S ESSENTIAL CONTRIBUTION WAS THE POSSIBILITY OF A LESS THAN FULL EMPLOYMENT EQUILIBRIUM, AND THE NEED FOR GOVERNMENT INTERVENTION TO MANAGE THE LEVEL OF DEMAND IN ORDER TO ACHIEVE FULL EMPLOYMENT.**

6.   Our initial analysis of the Keynesian Model **assumes that there is no taxation or government activity, a closed economy (i.e. no imports or exports) and no changes in the price level.** As a consequence **ALL INCOME** must be either **CONSUMED OR SAVED.** These simplifying assumptions will be dropped later.

7.   **THE CONSUMPTION FUNCTION** refers to the relationship between consumption (C) and income (Y). Research shows that income is the most important determinant of consumption, i.e.

$$C = f(Y) \ .$$

*where*
f = function of, or depends upon, income
C = consumption
Y = Income

If we drew a scatter diagram of an individual's consumption at different levels of income we would expect consumption to increase as income increases. This is illustrated in Diagram 12.1 by the observations plotted on the diagram. A line of best fit drawn through the observations i.e. C — C, is referred to as the **CONSUMPTION FUNCTION**. It can be observed that it is composed of a constant, a, and a slope or gradient, b, and if we assume a linear relationship (i.e. b is a constant) then the consumption function can be expressed as:

$$C = a + b(Y)$$

DIAGRAM 12.1

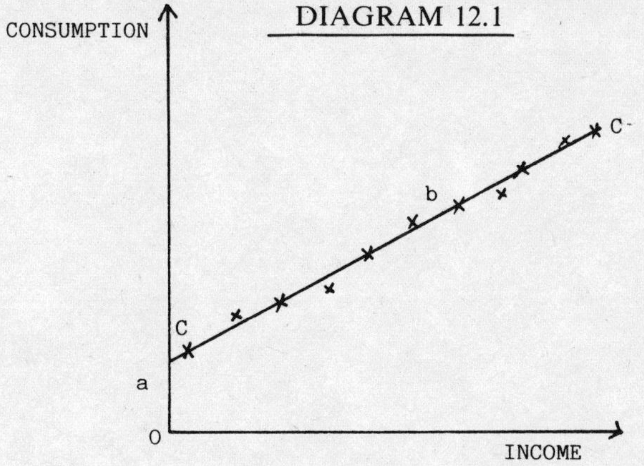

Where there are deductions from income in the form of taxation then consumption will depend upon the amount of **DISPOSABLE INCOME** i.e.

$$C = a + b(Yd)$$

where Yd = Disposable Income.

8.  A 45° line drawn from the origin indicates the points where **CONSUMPTION AND INCOME ARE EXACTLY EQUAL**. This is illustrated in Diagram 12.2(a) where the 45° line has been superimposed onto the consumption function. At the equilibrium point E all income is consumed. Below E consumption exceeds income and there is 'dis-saving', for example selling assets or living on earlier savings. Above E consumption is less than income and the area between CC and the 45° line represents savings. Ye is the equilibrium level of income. Diagram 12.2(b) illustrates the **SAVINGS FUNCTION** which corresponds with the pattern of consumption and saving in 12.2(a). When income is below Ye saving is negative, and above Ye it is positive, and because of the

relationship between consumption and saving both diagrams produce the same equilibrium level of income. Clearly it is **INCOME** which determines **CONSUMPTION** and **SAVING**.

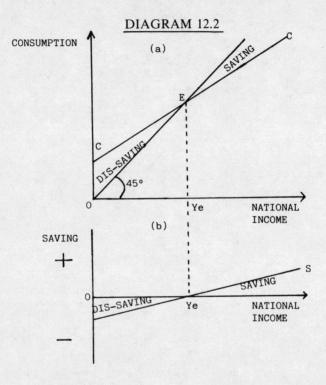

DIAGRAM 12.2

9.

9.1 The **MARGINAL PROPENSITY TO CONSUME (MPC)** refers to the amount of each additional unit of income which is consumed. It is calculated as:

$$\frac{\Delta C}{\Delta Y}$$

where C = consumption
Y = income
Δ = a small change

It is the MPC which determines the shape of the consumption function i.e. b in the formula C = a + b(Y).

9.2 The **MARGINAL PROPENSITY TO SAVE (MPS)** refers to the amount of each additional increment of income which is saved. It is calculated as:

$$\frac{\Delta S}{\Delta Y} \qquad \text{where } S = \text{saving}$$

9.3   Because income can only be either consumed or saved then:

$$\boxed{MPC + MPS = 1}$$

9.4   The **AVERAGE PROPENSITY TO CONSUME (APC)** and the **AVERAGE PROPENSITY TO SAVE (APS)** refer to the distribution of **TOTAL** income between consumption and saving and can be calculated for **EVERY** level of income. They are calculated as:

$$APC = \frac{C}{Y}$$

$$APS = \frac{S}{Y}$$

9.5   Table 12.1 below illustrates the calculation of both the MPC and the APC.

TABLE 12.1

| YEAR | INCOME (Y) | CONSUMPTION (C) | MPC $\frac{\Delta C}{\Delta Y}$ | APC $\frac{C}{Y}$ |
|------|-----------|-----------------|--------------------------------|-------------------|
| 1982 | 1000 | 800 | | .8 |
| 1984 | 1200 | 950 | $\frac{150}{200} = .75$ | .79 |

10.   The consumption behaviour described so far referred to the individual, however by **AGGREGATING EACH INDIVIDUAL'S CONSUMPTION FUNCTION** we can produce a similar consumption function for the **ECONOMY AS A WHOLE** relative to **NATIONAL INCOME**. There will also, therefore, be an MPC, MPS, APC and APS for the economy as a whole. From this point on therefore we will be referring to **TOTAL CONSUMPTION (TC)** and **NATIONAL INCOME (Y)**.

11.   Bearing in mind our assumptions regarding the closed economy and absence of government we can develop our conditions for

national income equilibrium. In our analysis so far we have assumed that the only expenditure is consumption (C). However we know from our national income analysis that investment (I) is also an element in total expenditure. It is reasonable to assume that investment, like consumption, rises with income, therefore in diagram 12.3 an **INVESTMENT SCHEDULE** (I) has been added. Aggregating the consumption and investment schedules produces the combined C + I schedule, to produce the equilibrium level of income Ye. In the lower diagram 12.3(b) this can be seen to be the same point as the intersection of the saving and investment schedules. The equilibrium condition for national income is therefore the point where the C + I line intersects the 45 °line; which is the same as saying that equilibrium is where income equals expenditure (E) i.e.

$$Y = E$$

at which point, as we can see from 12.3(b)

$$S = I$$

12. The equilibrium condition for national income **S = I** can be easily illustrated by the use of circular flow diagrams, as in Diagram 12.4. In period 1 firms are paying out factor incomes (national income) of £100m to households. The chain of respending is not complete however because only £80m goes directly back to firms in the form of consumption because there are **LEAKAGES** from the circular flow in the form of savings which amount to £20m. This would not matter if the **INJECTIONS** in the form of investment into the circular flow were also £20m.

DIAGRAM 12.4

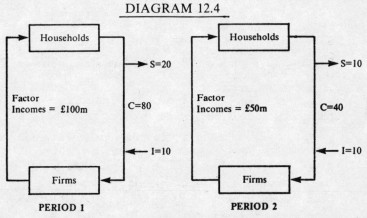

PERIOD 1            PERIOD 2

However, firms are only **PLANNING** to invest £10m, therefore total receipts by firms are reduced and they will be unable to pay out the same amount in factor payments in period 2. In period 2 factor payments to households fall to £90m, i.e. **NATIONAL INCOME FALLS.** Incomes continue to fall until households are no longer planning to save more than firms are attempting to invest and when savings and investment are again equal at £10m equilibrium is established with National Income = £50m. Had planned investment exceeded savings national income and therefore savings, would have risen until savings had risen sufficiently to match investment, again establishing equilibrium where **S = I.** (Assuming the MPC remains constant at 0.8).

13. According to Keynes therefore it was **FLUCTUATIONS IN NATIONAL INCOME AND THEREFORE EMPLOYMENT WHICH BROUGHT ABOUT EQUILIBRIUM BETWEEN INCOME AND EXPENDITURE, AND THIS EQUILIBRIUM COULD BE AT ANY LEVEL OF EMPLOYMENT.**

14. The equilibrium condition can also be explained in terms of national income analysis. From Chapter 1 we know that in equilibrium income (Y) is equal to expenditure (E).

*therefore* Y = E in equilibrium

As all income is either consumed (C) or saved (S), then

(1) Y = C + S

and as expenditure in our closed economy is either consumption or investment (I), then

(2) Y = C + I

As C can be eliminated from both equations 1 and 2, as it is common to both sides, we are left with the equilibrium condition

$$\boxed{S = I}$$

15. We can now drop our assumption of no government activity and introduce the third element of total demand **GOVERNMENT EXPENDITURE** (G). When government expenditure is added to the private expenditures of consumption and investment we can derive what is referred to as **AGGREGATE MONETARY DEMAND** (AMD), alternatively referred to as **EFFECTIVE DEMAND**.

$$\boxed{\textbf{AMD} = \textbf{C} + \textbf{I} + \textbf{G}}$$

### DIAGRAM 12.5

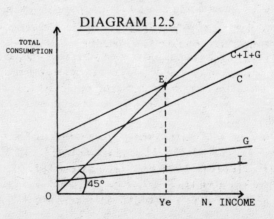

Diagram 12.5 illustrates the separate C, I and G schedules, which together constitute the aggregate monetary demand curve of C + I + G, giving the equilibrium of income and expenditure at E (income Ye).

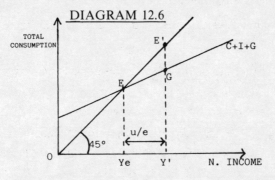

DIAGRAM 12.6

16.   As we have discussed earlier however there is in the Keynesian model no reason why the equilibrium point E should coincide with the full employment level of income. In diagram 12.6 equilibrium E produces level of income Ye but the level of income consistent with full employment is Y', and equilibrium point E', unemployment is therefore Ye — Y'. The deficiency of AMD at the full employment level is E' — G, known as the **DEFLATIONARY GAP**. The problem is therefore how to shift the equilibrium level of income from E to E', the full employment level.

17.   Shifting equilibrium output from E to E' could be achieved by an increase in investment, but this would be unlikely to occur autonomously (independently), as firms facing a depressed level of sales would have little incentive to invest. What Keynes argued was that governments should intervene in the economy and raise the level of their own expenditures on for example public works projects and boost the level of AMD to the full employment level. The increase in G would therefore represent an **INJECTION** into the circular flow of income.

18.   One essential point of the analysis is that the increase in G will not have to be as large as the required increase in AMD because of the **MULTIPLIER** process of respending. The simplest way to explain this respending process is to imagine an area of the country which has suffered high levels of unemployment and recession over a

sustained period. The government then decides to build a major highway between two towns in the region and spend many million of pounds on the project. The contract is placed with a construction company, however before they can proceed they have to place orders for new construction equipment and materials, the suppliers of this equipment and materials have to employ additional labour to produce it, this labour is now in receipt of wages and proceeds to spend them, local businesses find they are selling more and place orders for additional supplies, the suppliers of which take on fresh labour and so on. In addition the construction firm will take on new direct labour for construction purposes, these workers will now make increased expenditures with local traders. A cycle of re-spending is started and each pound spent by the government will have an effect on final demand which is some multiple greater than itself. This is referred to as the **MULTIPLIER PROCESS**.

19.   How large this multiplier process is depends upon how much is respent at each round, which is a function of the MPC and MPS of the income recipients. If they spend a high proportion of their incomes the multiplier will be larger than if a large proportion is saved at each round. The higher the MPC therefore the greater is the multiplier. This can be illustrated in Table 12.2 where the original government expenditure is £50, with an MPC of .7 and and MPS of .3.

## TABLE 12.2

| | INCOME (£) | CONSUMED (£) | SAVED (£) |
|---|---|---|---|
| 1st spending round | 50 | 35 | 15 |
| 2nd | 35 | 24.50 | 10.50 |
| 3rd | 24.50 | 17.50 | 7 |
| 4th | 17.50 | 12.00 | 5.50 |
| 5th | 12.00 | 8.40 | 3.60 |
| 6th | 8.40 | 5.88 | 2.52 |
| 7th | 5.88 | 4.10 | 1.78 |
| 8th | 4.10 | 2.88 | 1.22 |
| 9th | 2.88 | 2.00 | .88 |
| 10th | 2.00 | 1.40 | .60 |
| 11th | 1.40 | .98 | .42 |

The process continues until the amount of re-spending reduces to an infintely small amount, and the total amount of income generated, or the multiplier effect, will be £166.66. This consists of the original £50 of government expenditure, referred to as **AUTONOMOUS EXPENDITURE**; plus the re-spending generated at each successive round, referred to as **INDUCED EXPENDITURE**.

20.    The **MULTIPLIER** refers to the amount by which final income will be raised by any increase in government spending (or Investment). The multiplier coefficient (usually represented by k) can be calculated by the formula

$$k = \frac{1}{1 - MPC}$$

**OR** the **RECIPROCAL** of the MPS. (The mathematically inclined will identify Table 12.2 as a geometric progression, the sum of which is the formula.)

In order to illustrate, let us assume that National Income is £2000m and the government raises its expenditures by £50m, the effect on income is calculated as follows:

$$
\begin{aligned}
\text{National Income} &= \text{£2000m} \\
\Delta G &= \text{£50m} \\
MPC &= .7 \\
\textit{therefore } k &= \frac{1}{1 - .7} = 3.33
\end{aligned}
$$

$$50 \times 3.33 = 166.67$$
New National Income = **£2166.67m**

(Note it is only the injection of £50m which is subject to the multiplier.)

21.    The multiplier is illustrated in diagram 12.7. The economy is originally in equilibrium at E with income Y'. The full employment level of income is Yf, unemployment is Y' — Yf. An increase in G ( $\Delta$G) raises the AMD curve from E to the full employment

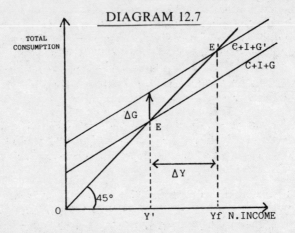

DIAGRAM 12.7

equilibrium E′ (income Yf). It should be noted that the increase in G is only about one third of the increase in Y, due to the effect of the multiplier. The effect of the multiplier can be estimated as

$$\frac{\Delta Y}{\Delta G}$$

22. As the size of the multiplier is dependent upon the MPC, and we know that the MPC is the same as b in the formula for the consumption function $C = a + b(Y)$, which is the slope of the curve,

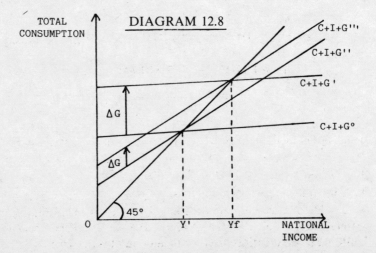

DIAGRAM 12.8

then graphically the steeper the slope of the AMD curve the greater the multiplier effect. In diagram 12.8 the increase in income from Y' to Yf was acheived by a much smaller increase in G when the AMD curve is steeper than when it has a shallow slope, this is because the steeper slope has a higher MPC (b) than the shallow slope, and the multiplier is correspondingly greater.

23. We can now **DROP OUR ASSUMPTION OF A CLOSED ECONOMY** and allow for the effects of **IMPORTS** and **EXPORTS** in the form of the Balance of Payments surplus or deficit.

24.

24.1 So far the only **INJECTIONS** into the circular flow have been **INVESTMENT (I)** and **GOVERNMENT EXPENDITURE (G)**. We can now add a third, **EXPORTS (X), as selling goods abroad is an injection of purchasing power into the domestic economy.**

**24.2 The only WITHDRAWAL** from the circular flow so far has been **SAVING (S)**. However as we have introduced government expenditure we must also allow for the effects of taxation **(T)**; and as we now have an 'open' economy, for the effects of **IMPORTS (M)** which reduce purchasing power in the domestic economy.

24.3

| Total INJECTIONS | = INVESTMENT | + GOVERNMENT EXPENDITURE | + EXPORTS |
|---|---|---|---|
| i.e. $J =$ | I | + G | + X |
| Total WITHDRAWALS = | SAVING | + TAXATION | + IMPORTS |
| i.e. $W =$ | S | + T | + M |

25. The **EQUILIBRIUM CONDITION** for national income now becomes

**INJECTIONS = WITHDRAWALS or**

$$\boxed{J = W}$$

which is identical to our previous closed economy condition of $S = I$ except that savings and investment are no longer the only injections and withdrawals from the circular flow.

26. In addition to the Marginal Propensities to Consume and Save we now have to accommodate the fact that some of any increment to income will be taken in **TAXATION** and some will be spent on **IMPORTS**, we therefore need to include in our analysis:

### 26.1 THE MARGINAL PROPENSITY TO IMPORT (MPM)
which is the amount of each increment to income which is spent on imports.

### 26.2 THE MARGINAL PROPENSITY TO TAX (MPT) which is
the amount of each increment to income which is taken in tax (the tax rate).

26.3   Note that the **MPC + MPS + MPM + MPT = 1**.

27.   We can illustrate the principle again by the use of simple circular flow diagrams.

DIAGRAM 12.9

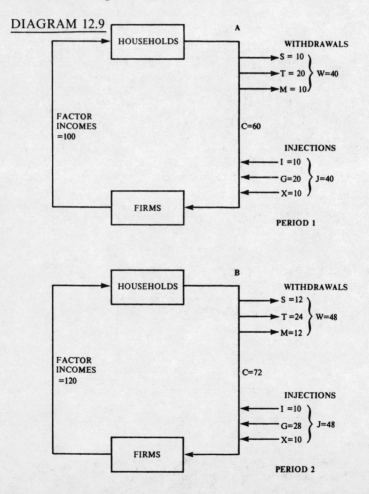

Diagram A represents an economy in equilibrium as the factor payments to households are received back by firms therefore **WITHDRAWALS ARE EQUAL TO INJECTIONS** i.e. J = W at £40m. It should also be noted that there is a Balance of Payments equilibrium (X = M) and the government has a balanced budget (G = T). Unemployment is however unacceptably high and it is estimated that the full employment income is £120m. In order to achieve this increase in income the government increases its expenditure by £8m which after the multiplier effect raises national income by £20m, a multiplier of 2.5. The government has achieved its full employment objective but note that this is only at the cost of "trading-off" other equally desirable objectives.

27.1   A deficit has emerged on the Balance of Payments (i.e. Imports = 12, Exports = 10.

27.2   The government now has a deficit on its budget (Taxation = 24) Government Expenditure = 28). This implies an increase in the **PUBLIC SECTOR BORROWING REQUIREMENT** which may have an inflationary impact on the price level.

27.3   There may be a fall in the exchange rate as a result of the Balance of Payments deficit which may add further inflationary pressure.

28.   The **MULTIPLIER** (k) is now calculated by the following:

$$k = \frac{1}{1 - MPC}$$

**OR**

$$\frac{1}{MPT + MPM + MPS}$$

e.g.  MPC = .6
MPM = .1
MPS = .1
MPT = .2

*therefore*   $k = \dfrac{1}{1 - .6} = \dfrac{1}{.4} = 2.5$

or   $k = \dfrac{1}{.2 + .1 + .1} = \dfrac{1}{.4} = 2.5$

29.   It is now possible to allow for an increase in AMD by an increase in either, or all, of the injections G, I or X. We will continue to assume however that the easiest of these variables for the government to manipulate is its own spending. Aggregate demand now however includes the effect of the **BALANCE OF PAYMENTS DEFICIT OR SURPLUS** (X — M), hence our AMD schedule now becomes:

$$AMD = C + I + G + (X - M)$$

For brevity we will now identify the C + I + G + (X — M) line as AMD.

30.   Previously we also utilised saving and investment functions, as these were the only withdrawals and injections, we can however follow the same analysis utilising an **INJECTIONS FUNCTION (J)** which represents I + G + X and a **WITHDRAWALS FUNCTION (W)** representing S + T + M. It is not unreasonable to assume that all these functions rise with income and, as we have already established, equilibrium is where J = W.

31.   We can illustrate the shift to a new equilibrium by utilising 45° line analysis as before or by using injections and withdrawals functions. In diagram 12.10 the economy is equilibrium at E with income Y below the full employment level Yf. In order to achieve full employment the government increases its expenditure, but it could be any of the injections G, I or X, i.e. Δ J. This has the desired multiplier effect and shifts the AMD line to E′, the size of the multiplier effect being

$$\frac{\Delta Y}{\Delta J}$$

and new equilibrium E′ is at the full employment level of income Yf. In 12.10 (ii) this is represented as a shift in the injections function (J). Original equilibrium is at E where J = W, the increased injections ( Δ J) shift J to J′ and income rises until a new equilibrium is established where J = W again at E′, and income Yf. The horizontal shift in Y being greater than the increase in G (i.e. Δ J) due to the multiplier effect, which can again be estimated as

$$\frac{\Delta Y}{\Delta J}$$

Exactly the same result could have been achieved by reducing withdrawals and in diagram 12.10 (iii) this is represented by a shift of the withdrawals function (W) down from W to W′ whilst injections remain constant. Income rises as a consequence and continues to do so until J = W again at E′ and income has risen from Y to Yf. The size of the multiplier effect being

$$\frac{\Delta Y}{\Delta W}$$

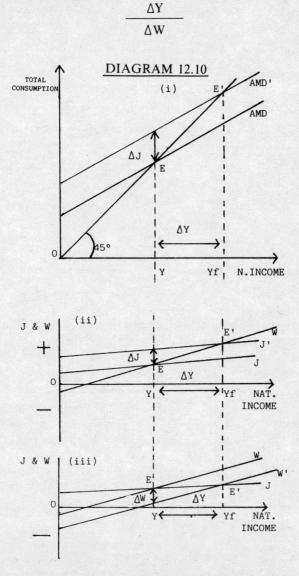

DIAGRAM 12.10

32. With the inclusion of the additional variables it is evident that there are other policy instruments available to the government in addition to its own expenditure which can be used to boost the level of demand, for example reductions in direct or indirect taxes, encouragement to private investment or assisting exports. It is more likely in fact to be a 'policy mix' rather than total reliance on a single policy instrument.

33. Policy measures are generally referred to as being either **FISCAL** or **MONETARY**.

33.1 **FISCAL POLICY** generally refers to changes in **GOVERNMENT EXPENDITURE** and **TAXATION**.

33.2 **MONETARY POLICY** generally refers to the control of the money supply (open market operations etc.), control of the banking system, and interest rate policy.

33.3 **DIRECT CONTROLS** operate directly upon the policy objective, e.g. Incomes Policy.

33.4 In reality the distinction between Fiscal and Monetary Policy is not quite so straightforward, for example the PSBR is one of the most important influences on the money supply but arises as a **CONSEQUENCE** of the level of government expenditure (fiscal policy).

34. In the analysis so far we have assumed that the multiplier is utilised to increase AMD during a period of deficient demand. The process could be reversed and in a period of excess demand the inflationary pressures reduced by selecting the appropriate policy mix of reduced government spending and increased taxation to produce a 'downward' multiplier effect. Experience indicates however that Keynesian policies have been less successful in dealing with inflation than unemployment.

35. Prior to Keynes the annual Budget was similar to a book-keeping exercise whereby the sources of tax revenue and how the government intended to spend it was outlined, and there was generally a belief that as far as possible the budget should balance. The implication of Keynes's analysis was that the government should deliberately aim for an unbalanced budget.

35.1 In a situation of deficient demand and recession the government should spend more than it gathers in tax revenue and run a **BUDGET DEFICIT**.

35.2   In a situation of excess demand and inflation a government may in theory attempt to gather more in taxation than it spends and run a **BUDGET SURPLUS**, although with the fixed commitments of modern governments this is unlikely in reality.

36.   Keynes advocated that the increased government spending could be financed by the government borrowing from wealth holders. The additional income created would generate sufficient tax revenue to repay the borrowing, and those finding employment would now be taxpayers rather than receivers of benefits. The process would not be inflationary provided domestic output could grow sufficiently rapidly. The additional borrowing does however imply an increase in the PSBR.

37.   Keynes's ideas were first tried in the U.S.A. with the 'New Deal' in 1933, where projects such as the Tennessee Valley Authority scheme were undertaken. Most countries however based the management of their economies on Keynesian principles in the period following 1945 until inflation became the overriding concern during the mid 1970's, and the emphasis changed towards the control of the money supply as being the most important policy instrument.


## SELF ASSESSMENT QUESTIONS

1.   What is the consumption function?

2.   What is the Marginal Propensity to Consume and how is it calculated?

3.   State the equilibrium condition for a closed economy with no government sector.

4.   State the components of aggregate monetary demand in an open economy with government activity.

5.   State the equilibrium conditions for an open economy with taxation and government spending.

6.   Given an MPC of .8 calculate the size of the multiplier.

# Chapter 13
# DEMAND MANAGEMENT IN PRACTICE

1.  The objectives of economic policy can be stated as:

    **1.1 FULL EMPLOYMENT**
    **1.2 STABLE PRICES**
    **1.3 BALANCE OF PAYMENTS EQUILIBRIUM**
    **1.4 ECONOMIC GROWTH**

In achieving any one of these objectives governments may have to accept a deterioration or 'trade-off' in one or more equally desirable policy targets.

2.  The use of Keynesian policies in the 1950's and 1960's prevented any return to the mass unemployment of the 1930's, the era was however characterised by what has been referred to as 'stop-go' policies as governments attempted to achieve their policy targets, but found them difficult to achieve simultaneously. Following Beveridge (1944) full employment was generally accepted to be about 3% unemployment. As unemployment rose above this figure measures would be taken to expand the economy by appropriate fiscal policy measures (government spending and taxation) in order to increase the level of economic activity and reduce unemployment. The increase in demand however also had the effect of increasing imports because not all of the additional demand was met from domestic output, and also of raising the price level which made U.K. exports less competitive, consequently a balance of payments deficit emerged. This put downward pressure on the exchange rate and under its commitment to maintain the exchange rate the government would be forced to intervene and use the foreign exchange reserves in support of sterling. The achievement of the full employment objective had been at the cost of price stability and the balance of payments. In order to stabilise the price level and eliminate the deficit on the balance of payments the government would then introduce deflationary policies in order to dampen down demand, the rate of price increase would stabilise and an improvement in the balance of payments would be achieved at the cost of higher unemployment, hence the reference to 'stop-go' policies. One of the arguments against the 'stop-go' cycle was that it created a climate of uncertainty

and therefore interfered with investment plans and reduced long term growth prospects. The period also saw repeated attempts to introduce **INCOMES POLICIES** which were intended to keep the rate of wage increase within the increase in productivity in order to allow the economy to be run closer to full employment whilst avoiding the inflationary effects. Unfortunately during the most stringent periods of incomes policy costs rose due to non wage factors, e.g. oil in 1973/74.

3.   The Keynesian model outlined in the previous chapter ignored any effect the increase in AMD may have had on the price level. In diagram 13.1(a) equilibrium is shifted from E to E', the full employment level, by an appropriate fiscal policy mix. In the lower diagram (b) however, it can be seen that prices are relatively stable until full resource utilisation is approached when they begin to rise progressively. At full employment output cannot be raised further and the rate of increase becomes almost vertical. Where there are

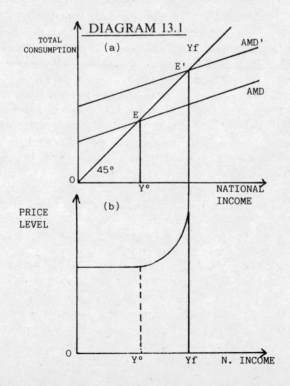

unemployed resources therefore a reflation of the economy through fiscal policy would initially raise real output and employment with a modest rise in the price level, but as full employment is approached further increases in demand result only in a rise in the rate of inflation.

4. The 'trade-off' between inflation and unemployment was formalised in the **PHILLIPS CURVE.** A.W. Phillips (1958), using data covering the period 1861-1957, identified a close correlation between the rate of change of money wages and employment. As wages are the most significant influence on prices the Phillips Curve can also be expressed as the relationship between inflation (rate of change of prices) and unemployment, as illustrated in diagram 13.2. On the curve rates of inflation can be identified for each level of unemployment. Stable wages should be achieved at $5\frac{1}{2}\%$ unemployment, and $2\frac{1}{2}\%$ unemployment for price stability. The employment target of 3% would be associated with a modest level of inflation, and as employment is reduced below this there is ever accelerating inflation. Very high levels of unemployment such as x may even be associated with falling prices (Y). Note that as the curve approaches full resources utilisation it becomes progressively steeper, hence at low levels of unemployment further reductions becomes more costly in terms of inflation. The Phillips Curve was very accurate in predicting wage increases over the period 1958-1966, however the concept of the Phillips Curve took a severe blow during the period 1974/75 when unemployment actually rose to $5\frac{1}{2}\%$ but rather than price stability price increases of over 20% were being recorded. (This is discussed further in Chapter 17).

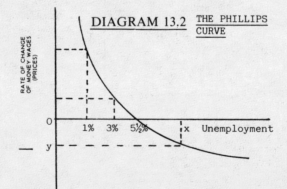

DIAGRAM 13.2 THE PHILLIPS CURVE

5.  Monetarists (see Chapter 16) also suggest that the budget deficits resulting from demand management policies and the increase in the Public Sector Borrowing Requirement that this implies results in an increase in the money supply and as a consequence leads to inflation.

6.

6.1   The use of government spending described in the Keynesian model is also criticised on the grounds that the government expenditure would merely replace or "**CROWD OUT**" an equivalent amount of private expenditure. Keynes suggested however that the multiplier effect would generate a sufficient increase in total expenditure to prevent this.

6.2   Crowding out may however happen as a result of the increase in interest rates which result from the budget deficit. In order to raise the necessary debt finance the government issues debt instruments (Treasury Bills and Gilts) which compete with the private demand for finance and raise the interest rate. The increase in the interest rate may reduce any private investment expenditures which are interest rate elastic (i.e. sensitive to interest rate changes). This implies that total expenditure may not increase by as much as the traditional multiplier suggests.

7.  The new phenomenon which arose in the mid 1970's of rising unemployment and simultaneously rising prices, referred to as **SLUMPFLATION** or **STAGFLATION** suggested that the previously accepted relationships had broken down and were difficult to accommodate within orthodox demand management policies. In particular the Keynesian tradition of demand manangement and the relationships explicit with the orthodox Phillips Curve came under attack. Some of the criticisms of the Keynesian model have been outlined above but these and the criticisms of the Phillips Curve will be discussed in more detail in later chapters.


## SELF ASSESSMENT QUESTIONS

1.  Outline the 'stop-go' cycle.

2.  Discuss the relationship between increases in aggregate demand and the price level.

3.  What are the implications for the relationship between prices and employment contained within the Phillips Curve?

4.  Why was the period of the mid 1970's referred to as an era of 'stagflation'?

5.  How might government spending 'crowd-out' private spending?

# Chapter 14
# THE ACCELERATOR

1.   The **ACCELERATOR** is a **CAPITAL STOCK ADJUSTMENT PROCESS** which relates changes in the capital stock to the **RATE OF CHANGE OF NATIONAL INCOME.**

2.   The demand for capital is a **DERIVED DEMAND**, as capital is not demanded for its own sake, but for what it will produce, it therefore reflects changes in consumer demand which is itself dependent upon income. The accelerator principle suggests that any change in income (consumption) will be reflected in a magnified form in the output of the capital goods industries.

3.   In order to illustrate this principle we will assume that in the production of brake cylinders for cars there is a fixed ratio between output and the number of lathes required (capital stock). If we assume that 10 lathes are required to produce 1000 cylinders and each lathe lasts for 10 years, as long as demand remains constant at 1000 cylinders each year the firm will just replace the one lathe which wears out each year. However if as a result of an increase in income demand rises to 1100 cylinders, an increase of 10%, the firm will now have to order 2 lathes, 1 replacement machine plus 1 to provide the additional capacity, therefore the demand for lathes, and therefore the output of the lathe industry, has risen by 100%. A 10% increase in consumption has resulted in a 100% increase in the output of the capital goods industry i.e. an "accelerated effect". If income continues to rise at 10% per annum then the output of both industries will continue to grow, however if eventually consumption ceases to grow and the firms supplying brakes and other components to the car industry find they have sufficient capital to meet current demand, investment demand will return to replacement demand and in the example the demand for lathes would return to 1 each year, a 50% fall in the output of the lathe industry, again an accelerated effect of the change in consumption but this time operating in reverse. A reduction in investment demand can therefore occur as a result merely of a failure of consumption to increase. If consumption actually declines then the firm may find it has excess capacity and may not even replace its worn out machines. This "naive"

accelerator provides one explanation for the pronounced cyclical upturns and downturns in the output of the capital goods industries.

4.   The "naive" or simple accelerator can be expressed as follows. If we assume a direct relationship between income (GDP) and the stock of capital required to produce it, then

$K = \alpha Y$

where  K  =   the stock of capital
       Y  =   income (GDP)
       $\alpha$  =   the coefficient (ratio) which
              relates the level of capital
              stock to the level of output.

Changes in the stock of capital are the same thing as investment therefore $\Delta K = I$, and

(2) $I = \alpha \cdot \Delta Y$      (or alternatively $I = \alpha \Delta C$)


5.   In reality the accelerator effect may not be as extreme as suggested in the example and the effect may be dampened by a number of factors.

   5.1   Firms will not automatically increase investment at the first sign of an increase in sales, they may prefer to wait until they become convinced that the increase in sales is permanent. They may rationalise that some loss in sales in the short-run is less expensive than a bad investment decision.

   5.2   There may be some excess capacity in the industry which can be utilised before new investment becomes necessary. It may even be possible to use existing capacity more intensively, for example by working extra shifts. Although this may raise costs it may still be cheaper than re-investing to meet a temporary increase in demand.

   5.3   The capital goods industries may not be able to respond quickly to an increase in demand and it may take a considerable time for them to adjust their own capacity.

6.   The accelerator may therefore be subject to considerable time lags. In order to incorporate these lags several other accelerator models have been developed, these lagged accelerator models can be found in most more advanced texts.

7. The accelerator principle may explain the upper and lower turning points of the trade cycle. If as a result of an increase in income there is an increase in investment and a growth in the output of the capital goods industries the additional investment will generate a multiplier effect on incomes and a further rise in consumption and further new investment. The accelerator and multiplier interacting with each other in an upward spiral. Eventually however the full employment ceiling will be reached and output cannot increase, or at least slows down. As the rate of growth of incomes slows down, or ceases, the accelerator effect operates in the opposite direction and the stabilising of consumption has a magnified downward effect on the capital goods industries. The reduction in investment has a downwards multiplier effect on consumption and multiplier and accelerator interact in a downward spiral into recession. If the economy has been in a prolonged recession with low levels of consumer demand, firms will eventually have to make a choice between reinvesting to worn out plant or going out of business. As plant becomes worn out or obsolete and firms are forced to reinvest they set the upward spiral in motion again. This of course is a highly simplified outline of the process, but does provide one explanation of the upper and lower turning points of the trade cycle.

## SELF ASSESSMENT QUESTIONS

1. What is the 'driving force' behind the accelerator principle?

2. Outline the relationship between changes in consumption and the output of the capital goods industries.

3. What factors may dampen the accelerator effect?

4. Explain how the accelerator and multiplier may interact in an upward or downward spiral.

# Chapter 15

## INTEREST RATE DETERMINATION

1.   The Marginal Productivity theory of interest rate determination was discussed in the companion volume of this text (Basic Concepts in Micro Economics) and should be referred to at this point. In this chapter we will briefly outline the Keynesian view of interest and money.

2.   We will consider first the relationship between interest rates and the firm's investment plans. A firm considering any investment proposal will attempt to estimate the addition to profits which will be forthcoming from the investment project. These additions to profit will not however be made in a single time period but will be received over several years. In order to estimate the net benefit of the investment it is necessary therefore to estimate the **NET PRESENT VALUE** of the future returns by means of a **DISCOUNT** factor. To explain this more simply, imagine the alternatives of £100 received today or £100 received in 1 year's time with a current interest rate of 10%. If the £100 received today had been invested for 1 year it would have been worth £110, alternatively we would only need to invest £91 today for it to be worth £100 in 1 year's time. Hence £100 in 1 year's time is worth only £91 today. In other words future income receipts are worth less than present income receipts. For this reason estimates of future income receipts from an investment project have to be **DISCOUNTED** by an appropriate **DISCOUNT RATE** in order to find the **PRESENT VALUE**, the process being similar to compound interest in reverse. The Discount Rate represents the **OPPORTUNITY COST OF CAPITAL**, which is in fact the **RATE OF INTEREST**; as the outlay involved in the project could have been invested and have earned interest with zero risk. The present value of the annual inflows is summed and compared with the cost of buying the machine (C), if the present value is greater than the cost the project goes ahead, and vice versa.

3.   This process, referred to as **DISCOUNTED CASH FLOW**, can be represented as

$$PV = \sum_{i=1}^{n} \frac{Y}{(1+r)n}$$

where   PV   =   Net Present Value

Y   =   Income or Yield from the investment

$\Sigma$   =   sum of

n   =   number of years the project will last

r   =   discount rate

Where PV is greater than C then the project should go ahead. (C = cost of buying the machine). If the PV were negative or zero the firm would be better off earning the current rate of interest in an alternative financial investment.

An alternative approach based on exactly the same principles as those outlined above is referred to as the **INTERNAL RATE OF RETURN** (IRR). This can be summarised as

$$PV = \sum_{i=1}^{n} \frac{Y}{(1 \times x)n} \qquad \text{where } x = IRR$$

The firm estimates the value of x (the internal rate of return) which produces a present value equal to the cost of the machine, i.e. finds that x which produces PV = C . The firm will rationally invest in the machine whenever the **INTERNAL RATE OF RETURN IS GREATER THAN THE RATE OF INTEREST** i.e. x is greater than r.

4. The Internal Rate of Return is also referred to as the **MARGINAL EFFICIENCY OF CAPITAL** (MEC). It will pay a firm to invest and increase its stock of capital up to the point where the MEC is equal to the interest rate.

5. If however the stock of capital is increased, relative to other factors, then like the other factors of production it will be subject to **DIMINISHING MARGINAL PRODUCTIVITY**. As a consequence the MEC declines as the capital stock is increased, and if represented diagramatically it slopes downwards to the right and constitutes the firm's **DEMAND CURVE FOR CAPITAL**. It slopes downwards because the most profitable investments will be undertaken first and further investments will be less profitable as marginal productivity declines, and will therefore only be undertaken at lower rates of interest. The profit maximising firm will be in equilibrium regarding its capital stock when the **MARGINAL EFFICIENCY OF CAPITAL IS EQUAL TO THE RATE OF INTEREST,** i.e.

MEC = R

In diagram 15.1 the firm is in equilibrium at E with capital stock Q when the rate of interest is R.

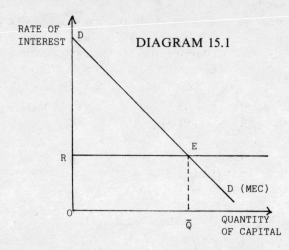

DIAGRAM 15.1

The firm would only increase its stock of capital if:

5.1 The Rate of Interest fell.

5.2 The MEC of capital increased, through for example the introduction of new technology.

6. We have so far taken the rate of interest as given, however in order to consider how the rate of interest is determined it is necessary to consider the demand for money. The demand for money does not refer to the demand for money for spending on goods, but the demand for the actual stock of money to hold as money balances. It will be recalled from Chapter 12 that according to 'Classical Theory' money was only held for purposes of making transaction and bridging the time period between income receipts, however Keynes added the possibility of the demand for money as an asset i.e. speculative balances. Three 'motives' for demanding money balances are identified as:

6.1 **TRANSACTIONS DEMAND** — as in Classical Theory transactions balances were needed to bridge the time gap between income receipts and expenditure. The size of such balances is dependent upon:

(i) The **LENGTH OF TIME** between receipts and expenditure.
(ii) The **SIZE** of receipts and expenditure. Transactions balances would vary with income and **NOT** rates of interest.

6.2 **PRECAUTIONARY DEMAND** — money will be held for the purpose of meeting unforseen emergencies. This motive was not included in Classical Theory where perfect certainty was assumed. Keynes grouped transactions and precautionary balances together into a single sum which varied directly with the **LEVEL OF INCOME**.

6.3 **SPECULATIVE DEMAND** — the speculative motive was Keynes's innovation. In order to understand this motive it is necessary to ask, why would people hold money balances over and above those described above when money is an asset which yields no return at all? The answer to this is that if other financial assets, in particular bonds, are likely to fall in price then losses on bonds can be avoided by holding money instead. The motive for holding speculative money balances was therefore to avoid losses in a declining securities market. In order to understand this more clearly it is necessary to consider the relationship between bond prices and the rate of interest. In this context Keynes was referring to undated government securities (referred to as 'Gilts' or 'Consols'). These bonds pay a fixed annual sum and are bought and sold on the securities market, their price therefore varies with demand and supply. For example if an undated security has a nominal value of £200 and pays £10 per annum the yield is 5%, i.e. the rate of interest is 5% as yield and the interest rate on a fixed interest bond are the same thing, e.g.

| MARKET PRICE | ANNUAL PAYMENT | (YIELD) RATE OF INTEREST |
|---|---|---|
| £400 | £10 | 2½% |
| £200 | £10 | 5% |
| £100 | £10 | 10% |

It can be seen that as the market price rises to £400 the fixed annual payment of £10 is only a 2½% rate of interest and when the price falls to £100 the rate of interest rises to 10%. The market price and rate of interest on fixed interest bonds is therefore **INVERSELY RELATED**.

7. Speculative money balances vary therefore with the anticipated gains or losses on the securities market, and the extent to which individuals prefer holdings of money to other financial assets is referred to as **LIQUIDITY PREFERENCE**. Bearing in mind the relationship between security prices and interest rates above we can make the following assumptions.

7.1   When security prices are high (and interest rates are low) speculators will expect bond prices to fall and therefore a capital loss to be made. They will therefore attempt to avoid such losses by holding speculative money balances. Low interest rates therefore imply a high liquidity preference. Note also that the opportunity cost of holding money is lower.

7.2   When bond prices are low (and interest rates therefore are high) speculators will anticipate a rise in bond prices and therefore a capital gain. They will attempt to take advantage of the capital gain on bonds by holding bonds rather than money balances. High interest rates therefore imply a low liquidity preference. Note also that the opportunity cost of holding money is higher.

8.   It is important to note the importance of speculators' expectations about the future course of interest rates. Each individual is assumed to hold his expectations with complete certainty, although there may be disagreement between individuals about the future course of interest rates.

9.   If each individual's liquidity preference is added together a **LIQUIDITY PREFERENCE CURVE** can be drawn, which represents the **DEMAND FOR MONEY**. The liquidity preference curve relates the total demand for money to the rate of interest. Although each individual may have different expectations of future events, by adding them all together we obtain the smooth liquidity preference curve in diagram 15.2.

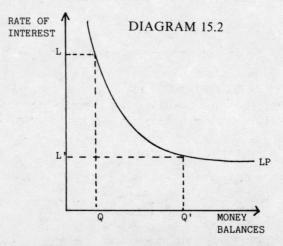

DIAGRAM 15.2

In diagram 15.2 when the interest rate is L bond prices will be low and a rise in bond prices, and therefore capital gains, will be anticipated and speculative balances will be zero, only transactions and precautionary balances being held i.e. Q. When the rate of interest is low at L' and bond prices are high capital losses are anticipated and larger speculative money balances are held i.e. Q' in order to avoid capital losses on bonds. The horizontal portion of the liquidity preference curve is referred to as the **LIQUIDITY TRAP**. In this portion of the curve the demand for money is infinitely elastic with respect to the interest rate. Reductions in the interest rate, in this portion only, increases people's desire to hold cash balances. The implication here is that any attempt to achieve internal expansion through increased investment brought about by lowering the interest rate would fail, because any increase in the money supply created in order to reduce the rate of interest would be held in the form of cash balances, making it impossible to use interest rates (monetary policy) to expand the economy.

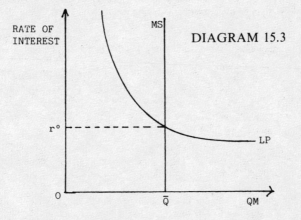

10. The **SUPPLY OF MONEY** at any point of time is fixed by the monetary authorities and is therefore independent of the rate of interest. In diagram 15.3 the money supply is therefore the vertical line MS. The rate of interest is determined where the demand for money (LP) intersects the supply (MS), at interest rate $r^\circ$.

Changes in the interest rate could occur as a result of:

10.1 A shift in the Liquidity Preference Curve as a result of anticipated changes in bond prices.

10.2 A shift in the money supply curve by the authorities changing the supply of money. Note that an increase in the horizontal portion, the liquidity trap, would leave interest rates unchanged and would be held entirely in the form of additional money balances making monetary policy weak and ineffectual.

11. Keynes suggested that the investment decisions by firms were only marginally influenced by interest rates, the major factor being **SALES EXPECTATIONS**. Firms would invest if they expected the future level of demand and therefore profits to be high.

12.

12.1 In classical theory the rate of interest brings equality between savings and investment; however in Keynesian theory savings and investment are brought into balance through changes in income operating through the multiplier process.

12.2 Keynesian theory emphasises the effect of interest rates on real activity through the effects on investment, and through the multiplier effect, on income.

12.3 Monetarists (see Chapter 16) stress the effects of interest rates on the money supply and inflation.

13. The interest rate here refers to the basic rate of interest on government undated bonds. There is of course a whole spectrum of other interest rates, e.g.

> Building Societies
> Hire Purchase
> Bank Deposit Accounts
> Private Tenders etc.

Each will have a different rate of interest which is determined by factors such as:

13.1 The duration of the loan.

13.2 The degree of risk, in particular the creditworthiness of the borrower.

13.3 Amount of collateral available.

13.4 Purpose and nature of the loan.

## SELF ASSESSMENT QUESTIONS

1. What is meant by the marginal efficiency of capital?

2. How does the firm determine its optimal stock of capital?

3. Discuss why the speculative demand for money varies with the rate of interest.

4. What is meant by liquidity preference?

5. How does liquidity preference and the money supply determine the rate of interest?

# Chapter 16
# MONETARISM & INFLATION

1.   The expression 'Monetarist' is a general term used to describe those economists who believe that the money supply is the most important factor in determining the level of expenditure and prices.

2.   The monetarist concepts have their origins in classical economics, however their revival in modified form owes much to Professor Milton Friedman. Friedman and Schwarts (A.J.) analysed data in the U.S.A. between 1867 and 1960 and demonstrated a close correlation (relationship) between changes in the money supply and the rate of change of money GDP, and therefore prices, after a time lag of about 18 months. Friedman suggested therefore that there was a strong causal relationship between the supply of money and inflation.

3.   Friedman states that "inflation is always and everywhere a monetary phenomenon", meaning that inflation is always due to an excessive growth in the money supply. Several historical examples are quoted such as the influx of gold from S. America into Europe in the 16th Century, the gold finds in California in 1849, and those in Australia and S. Africa in the late 19th and early 20th centuries: all of which were followed by a rapid rise in prices. Friedman suggests that those examples have their modern counterparts in the budget deficits of the second half of the 20th century.

4.   As inflation is caused only by increasing the money supply the implication is that as only governments can print money, then only governments cause inflation. Only governments therefore can cure inflation — by keeping a tight control over the supply of money. Governments can always obtain the resources they require by increasing the supply of money which raises the price level. The increase in the price level reduces real incomes which enables the government to acquire a greater share of the available resources. This is identical to the effect of taxation, hence Friedman refers to expansion of the money supply as "taxation without representation".

5.   The increase in the money supply arises from the budget deficits which governments maintain in order to pursue fiscal policies which

will maintain aggregate demand at levels consistent with full employment. Governments are pressed to maintain high levels of expenditure but they are unwilling to raise taxation in order to pay for it and so resort to deficit financing. (See Chapter 12). As suggested above, this is a hidden form of taxation due to the effect on the price level and therefore real incomes.

6.   At this stage it is worth reiterating exactly what we mean by the money supply. The most important definition in this context is Sterling M3 (£M3) which it wil be recalled from Chapter 10 is defined as:

Notes and Coins in Circulation + Current and Deposit accounts held by all U.K. residents in Sterling.

6.1   The money supply therefore includes not only notes and coin but also the banks' ability to create credit. An important element of controlling the money supply is therefore control of the banks' ability to create deposits.

6.2   It will be recalled from Chapter 10 that an increase in the government's budget deficit implies an increase in the public sector borrowing requirement (PSBR). The PSBR is financed by borrowing through the sale of gilts to the public and by the taking up of short term public sector debt (bills) by the banks which increases the asset base of the banks as these securities constitute bank reserve assets. This enables the banks to undertake the multiple expansion of credit, which represents an increase in £M3; 85% of which is comprised of bank deposits. Diagram 16.1 illustrates the link between government expenditure and the money supply.

## DIAGRAM 16.1

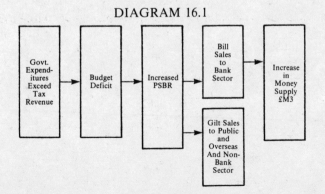

6.3   The government may attempt to sell as much of its debt as possible outside the banking system, to the public or other financial institutions, but in order to do this it will have to increase interest rates in order to attract them. To prevent an increase in the money supply by this method therefore implies a higher level of interest rates.

7.   Monetarists consider that the main reason for the increase in the money supply, and therefore inflation, is the commitment of governments to full employment. Governments have attempted to keep unemployment below the 'NATURAL RATE' of unemployment (see Chapter 17) and in order to achieve this have incurred ever increasing budget deficits, with the consequent growth in the money supply. Any attempt to keep unemployment below the natural rate will therefore result in ever increasing inflation (see Chapter 17).

8.   Essentially the monetarist view represents a return to the QUANTITY THEORY OF MONEY (see Chapter 9). It will be recalled that the Quantity Theory stated that

$$MV = PT$$

where M = Money Supply (£M3)
V = the velocity (or speed) of circulation of money
P = the price level
T = the level of transactions

The level of transactions (T) can be assumed to be the equivalent of the real level of economic activity or output.

9.   The debate between monetarists and Keynesians hinges around V, monetarists suggest it is a constant and therefore is predictable. Keynesians argue that it varies in an unpredictable manner with changes in interest rates (see Liquidity Preference Theory, Chapter 15). If we accept the monetarist contention that V is constant then any increase in M will result in an increase in the value of PT, and monetarists argue that the effect will fall on P (the price level) rather than T (real ouput), and will therefore be INFLATIONARY, i.e. EXCESSIVE GROWTH OF THE MONEY SUPPLY WILL INCREASE MONEY GDP (PRICES) RATHER THAN REAL GDP (OUTPUT).

10.   It will be recalled from Chapter 12 that in Keynesian economics an increase in the money supply will influence income only

**INDIRECTLY** through the reduction in the interest rate stimulating investment which would raise income through the multiplier effect. If there were unemployed resources in the economy output and real income would be raised; if there was full employment the price level would increase. In Keynesian economics therefore changes in the money supply affect the economy in an unpredictable and indirect manner and is therefore not a good policy instrument.

11. The monetarist transmission mechanism through which increases in the money supply result in higher expenditure is quite straightforward. Money is considered to be an imperfect substitute for other financial assets and is held for its own sake. When there is an increase in the money stock the immediate effect is that people find they are holding higher money balances in relation to their holdings of other assets than they desire. They therefore attempt to reduce their money balances and increase their holdings of other assets — a kind of 'portfolio' adjustment. Some of these additional money balances will be used to purchase other forms of financial assets, however some will be used to purchase goods and services which are also considered to yield a return to the purchaser. The increased expenditures will result in higher prices.

12.

12.1 Monetarists believe that Fiscal Policy is a destabilising influence on the economy and should be avoided. This is because of the long and variable time lags between the implementation of a policy and its effect upon the economy. For example a reflationary policy taken during recession may take two years to take effect, by which time the economy may be growing autonomously and the effect of the policy becomes inflationary.

12.2 They believe that intervention in the economy should be minimal and that a simple monetary rule should be followed. A target rate of growth for the money supply should be announced which is consistent with the rate of growth of real output (GDP). Attempts by the workforce to gain wage increases which are not consistent with the rate of growth of the money supply can only result in higher unemployment. Workers are expected to learn from their experiences and as reduced monetary targets are anounced they will revise their expectations of inflation downwards and settle for lower wage increases.

13. The 1979 Conservative government embraced the Monetarist doctrine which was embodied within the 1980 **MEDIUM TERM FINANCIAL STRATEGY** (MTFS). The MTFS contained two key elements:

(i) A set of declining targets over a four year period for the growth of £M3.

(ii) A plan for the reduction of the PSBR as a proportion of GDP from 4.8% in 1979/80 to 1.5% by 1983/84.

14. The implication of the adoption of the MTFS is a switch of emphasis away from maintaining full employment to the control of inflation. The effect of the policy will be more expensive in terms of unemployment the more slowly workers revise their expectations of inflation, and therefore wage demands, downwards in the light of announced targets for monetary growth. In this context it is important that the government should be seen to be achieving its targets, which is not easy given the nature of broad aggregates such as £M3.

15.

15.1 One of the major criticisms of this strategy is that reductions in the money supply fall not on the price level (P) but on real output (T). The resulting decline in real output and activity results in high unemployment. It is this induced recession which critics suggest controls the price level rather than by any direct effect of the money supply on prices.

15.2 Keynesians suggest that if GDP is growing attempts to control the money supply will be by-passed by the development of alternative forms of money.

15.3 The results of research, such as that of Friedman, is criticised because the demonstration of a close correlation between the money supply and changes in GDP is not necessarily causal, and if GDP was growing the money supply could be expected to grow in line with it.

16. Monetarists advocate a reduced role for the state:

16.1 They believe that intervention through Keynesian type demand management policies are ineffective in reducing unemployment and result in inflation.

16.2    The production of as many goods and services as possible should be carried out by the private sector which is believed to be more efficient and more able to respond to consumers' needs.

17.    In very basic terms the monetarist view can be summarised as:

## CAUSE OF INFLATION

17.1    Governments spend more than they collect in tax revenue.

17.2    The increased expenditures by governments end up in people's pockets.

17.3    People find they are holding excess money balances so increase their expenditures.

17.4    The price level rises.

## CURE

17.5    Government reduces its deficit by cutting spending (on roads, schools etc.).

17.6    Less money in people's pockets.

17.7    People reduce their expenditures on goods and services.

17.8    The demand for goods falls so employers reduce the size of their workforce.

17.9    Employers now have smaller workforces and greater productivity, so costs fall/stabilise.

17.10    Prices stabilise: inflation cured **BUT** unemployment high.

(Note. This summary is not meaningful without the theoretical background outlined.)

## SELF ASSESSMENT QUESTIONS

1.    What is meant by "taxation without representation"?

2.    Describe how an increase in the PSBR implies an increase in the money supply.

3.    How is the commitment to 'full employment' connected with increases in the PSBR?

4.    What assumptions are implied by monetarists regarding the velocity of circulation of money (V)?

5. Outline the monetarist transmission mechanism by which increases in the money supply result in higher expenditures and prices.

6. Outline the monetarist rule for the growth of the money supply.

7. Why is it considered necessary to announce targets for monetary growth?

# APPENDIX

## The Monetarist Consumption Function and the Permanent Income Hypothesis

*This appendix is optional for A level students but would be useful to more advanced students.*

1.   Post-war cross sectional data on the consumption function has consistently provided a poor fit to that forecast on the basis of long-run time series data. Friedman's **PERMANENT INCOME HYPOTHESIS** provides one possible solution to this problem. The central theme of Friedman's theory is that **PLANNED OR PERMANENT CONSUMPTION** is proportional to expected or **PERMANENT INCOME**. Permanent income itself is dependent upon the individual's stock of wealth and subjective rate of interest (not market rate). Permanent income can be viewed as the annual flow of income generated by the individual's estimated stock of wealth at a rate equal to the rate of interest. Alternativelty, it is the annual flow of resources that could be spent by the individual without disturbing his estimated stock of wealth. Both permanent income and permanent consumption differ from measured income and consumption by amounts Friedman calls **TRANSITORY INCOME** and **TRANSITORY CONSUMPTION**. Current measured consumption (C) is the sum of transitory consumption (CT) and permanent consumption (CP), and current measured income (Y) is the sum of transitory income (YT) and permanent income (YP). The relation can be summarised as

*(MEASURED)* C = CP + CT
*(MEASURED)* Y = YP + YT
CP = kYP (k = factor of proportionality)

2.   Friedman also assumes that there is no systematic relationship or correlation between permanent income and transitory income, between consumption and transitory consumption.

3.   Friedman's version of the **CONSUMPTION FUNCTION** therefore differs significantly from the simple relationship between consumption and disposable income described in Chapter 12. In this version of the consumption function consumption depends upon **TOTAL RESOURCES AVAILABLE**. Resources are assumed to

include income from non-human wealth (i.e. property) plus income from human wealth (future earnings). The relationship described above between **PERMANENT CONSUMPTION** (Cp) and **PERMANENT INCOME** (Yp) is the basis of the consumption function which can be summarised in the equation:

$$Cp = k \, (i, w, u) \, Yp$$

3.1   The subjective rate of interest, i, at which the consumer can borrow or lend (not the market rate)

3.2   The relative importance of property and non property income, symbolised by the ratio of non-human wealth to income (w) and

3.3   The factors symbolised by the portmanteau variable u determining the consumer's tastes and preferences for consumption versus additions to wealth.

Consumption here refers to the **FLOW OF SERVICES** which goods yield over their lifetime, not the initial expenditure, since utility is derived from their services, not from the expenditure. For example a refrigerator will yield a service to the purchaser over its lifetime, say 10 years; in this sense it is therefore 'consumed' over 10 years.

4.   The essential point is that changes in income that are believed to be temporary do not cause the individual to revise his estimates of permanent income. **Also** unexpected or transitory changes in consumption spending cause no alteration or modification to permanent consumption expenditures.

**THE MPC OUT OF TRANSITORY INCOME IS ZERO.**

5.   The implication is that sudden or "windfall" changes as a result of Government Fiscal Policy may not have the predicted effect upon levels of consumption. Thus the multiplier effect of a tax reduction will be much lower than originally thought (or zero). The concept of transitory income provides one explanation for the poor fit of post-war consumption data to estimated consumption. This is illustrated in diagram 16.2.

Permanent consumption function is plotted through the origin i.e. CP. Suppose income falls Yo to Y1 and households perceive this fall to be transitory with no change in YP. Since there is no correlation between CT and YT and because permanent income has not changed

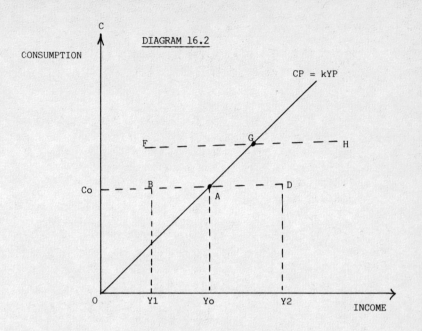

DIAGRAM 16.2

measured consumption will therefore not change. Thus for the fall in measured income from Yo to Y1 measured consumption remains constant at Co. The same is true of an increase Yo to Y2, giving the same consumption Co. Observed points from data would trace the line B.A.D. A consumption function fitted to these observations would not be the 'true' consumption-function. An increase in income which persisted long enough to be considered as permanent would result in a move from A to G, but there would then be a new 'short run' consumption function FGH. Successive points such as A and G produce the long run consumption function. The discrepancy between long run and short run observations is therefore explained by the fact that cross section, or short run data are observing short run consumption functions as BAD and FGH, whilst long run data are observing points such as A and G on the long run function.

# Chapter 17

## THE NATURAL RATE OF UNEMPLOYMENT & THE PHILLIPS CURVE

1.    The concept of the **NATURAL RATE OF UNEMPLOYMENT** is closely associated with the monetarist school of thought, and has much in common with the classical view of the labour market. It differs from the Keynesian view in that it considers unemployment from the **SUPPLY** side of the economy rather than resulting from deficient demand.

2.    The labour market is considered to be like any other market where the equilibrium price, which in this instance is the wage rate, is determined by demand and supply. The amount of labour demanded by employers will depend upon the level of **REAL WAGES**

$$\text{REAL WAGES} = \frac{\text{MONEY WAGES}}{\text{PRICES}} = \left( \frac{W}{P} \right)$$

the higher the real wage the lower the demand for labour, and vice versa. The total supply of labour will increase as the real wage rises and fall as the real wage falls. Provided the market operates smoothly then an equilibrium real wage will be established where the demand and supply for labour is equal. Any unemployment remaining when the labour market is in equilibrium is referred to as the **NATURAL RATE OF UNEMPLOYMENT**.

In diagram 17.1 DD is the demand curve for labour which slopes downwards reflecting the declining marginal productivity of labour. SS is the supply curve which slopes upwards indicating that at higher real wages more labour will be supplied. The labour market is in equilibrium at E with real wage $(W/P)^2$ and $Q_L E$ labour. If the real wage was above the equilibrium wage, for example at $(W/P)^1$ the quantity of labour demanded would fall to $Q_L^1$ but $Q_L^2$ would be supplied, there is therefore an excess supply of labour at this higher real wage and $Q_L^1 - Q_L^2$ will be unemployed at the prevailing real wage rate. Full employment could be restored by reducing real wages, for example by cutting money wages, this would increase the demand for labour and eliminate some of the excess supply returning

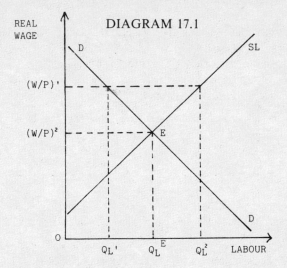

REAL WAGE

DIAGRAM 17.1

the labour market to equilibrium at E. The implication being that unemployment such as $Q_L^1$ — $Q_L^2$ is caused by real wages being too high and therefore the cure is to accept cuts in real wages. It follows therefore that any unemployment above $Q_LE$ is **VOLUNTARY** and occurs because workers are not willing to work for a low enough wage. $Q_LE$ is referred to as the **NATURAL RATE OF UNEMPLOYMENT** and is the **UNEMPLOYMENT WHICH REMAINS WHEN THE LABOUR MARKET IS IN EQUILIBRIUM.**

3.   Advocates of the natural rate consider that full employment as defined in the post-war era (3% in the U.K.) was a political objective rather than an economic concept. The natural rate of unemployment is the level the labour market would tend towards if wages were flexible and in the absence of artificial 'frictions' or obstacles.

4.   The natural rate of unemployment cannot be defined as some percentage of the labour force as it is not a constant. It depends upon a number of factors which are liable to change:

4.1   Technology and innovation.
4.2   Comparative advantage and international trade.
4.3   The degree of occupational and geographical mobility.
4.4   Information regarding job opportunities.
4.5   Restrictive practices imposed by Trade Unions.

5.   If unemployment is persistently high and above what may be considered the natural rate, according to this theory it is because the labour market is being prevented from operating smoothly and efficiently by the existence of 'frictions' or obstacles to supply. There are two main sources of such frictions which are suggested:

5.1   The high level of benefit paid to the unemployed which prevents them from taking low paid jobs. Professor Minford suggests a combination of reduced benefits and lower taxation as an incentive to the unemployed to take lower paid jobs. He suggests this disincentive effect is felt most strongly in the non-unionised sector of the workforce.

5.2   The power of trade unions to resist reductions in real wages and impose minimum wage rates prevents people from obtaining jobs at lower pay which they might otherwise take.

Both are areas which are highly controversial politically.

6.   Monetarists suggest that any attempt by governments to keep the level of unemployment below the natural rate will result in ever accelerating inflation. This has important implications for the Phillips Curve which it will be recalled from Chapter 13 implied a stable 'trade-off' between prices and employment. Governments could select a level of inflation and engineer the appropriate level of unemployment. However the Phillips Curve relationship started to break down towards the end of the 1960's and by the mid 1970's seemed to have broken down altogether, underpredicting the inflation rate by about 20%. Table 17.1 shows the change in retail prices and unemployment over the period 1960 to 1983.

7.   By 1976 instead of $5\frac{1}{2}\%$ unemployment giving the predicted wage stability it was associated with inflation of almost 25%. It was possible that the relationship had broken down altogether. An alternative suggestion was that the curve had shifted to the right, to PC2 in diagram 17.2, so that $5\frac{1}{2}\%$ unemployment was now associated with 25% inflation, and stable wages would now only be achieved at much higher levels of unemployment, such as y. The implication being that policies designed to stabilise inflation by reducing expenditure would now result in much higher unemployment levels than previously. Various reasons have been put forward for this apparent breakdown in the Phillips relationship but the fact that governments resorted to

## TABLE 17.1

| Year | Unemployment (UK Excl. N. Ireland) | Change in Retail Prices (%) |
|------|-----------------------------------|----------------------------|
| 1960 | 1.5  | 1.0  |
| 61   | 1.3  | 3.4  |
| 62   | 1.8  | 2.6  |
| 63   | 2.2  | 2.1  |
| 64   | 1.6  | 3.3  |
| 65   | 1.3  | 4.8  |
| 66   | 1.4  | 3.9  |
| 67   | 2.2  | 2.5  |
| 68   | 2.3  | 4.7  |
| 69   | 2.3  | 5.4  |
| 70   | 2.5  | 6.4  |
| 71   | 3.3  | 9.4  |
| 72   | 3.6  | 7.1  |
| 73   | 2.6  | 9.2  |
| 74   | 2.5  | 16.1 |
| 75   | 3.9  | 24.2 |
| 76   | 5.2  | 16.5 |
| 77   | 5.7  | 15.8 |
| 78   | 5.6  | 8.3  |
| 79   | 5.3  | 13.4 |
| 80   | 6.7  | 18.0 |
| 81   | 10.4 | 11.9 |
| 82   | 11.7 | 8.6  |
| 83   | 12.4 | 4.6  |
| 84   | 12.6 | 5.0  |
| 85   | 13.1 | 6.1  |

*Source: Economic Trends*

incomes policies at that time would suggest that they considered that wages and therefore costs were the most important factor. The view that cost increases were responsible operates within the traditional framework of the Phillips Curve and has two main elements:

7.1   The first is that prices rose due to cost-push inflation. This was associated with an increase in Trade Union militancy whereby Trade Unions were able to gain pay increases for their members which were greater than the rate of increase of productivity. Firms' costs would then rise and as a consequence prices would also rise. The increase in prices would reduce demand, resulting in increased unemployment and the simultaneous rise in prices and unemployment implies a worsening of the terms of the trade-off, and therefore the shift to the right of the curve to PC2 (diagram 17.2). If the government then attempts to increase aggregate demand in order to reduce unemployment there will be a further rise in inflation from a point such as x in diagram 17.2 to a point such as z with its high rate of inflation. This explanation sees the ability of Trade Unions to gain wage increases for their members above the rate of productivity increase even when unemployment is high, and the market power of firms to pass on these increases as being the main reason for the shift.

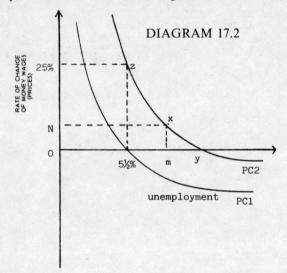

DIAGRAM 17.2

7.2 This explanation also incorporates the external cost increases, such as the oil price rises and the commodity price boom of the 1970's, as being of major significance in the process.

7.3 It also includes the possibility of higher benefits making the unemployed more selective about which jobs they take and an unwillingness to accept the lowest paid jobs.

8. Friedman criticised the original Phillips Curve on the grounds that it assumed that the **ANTICIPATED** rate of inflation was given, and also that the effect of **EXPECTATIONS** on inflation had been omitted; in which case the stable Phillips Curve relationship was only a very **SHORT-RUN** phenomenon. In the longer run there was no stable relationship and **ANY ATTEMPTS BY GOVERNMENT TO REDUCE UNEMPLOYMENT BELOW THE NATURAL RATE WOULD RESULT IN ACCELERATING INFLATION AND THE RETURN OF UNEMPLOYMENT TO THE NATURAL RATE.** The orthodox Phillips Curve assumes that workers suffer from a

**"MONEY ILLUSION"** i.e. the belief that an increase in money wages is the same as an increase in real wages. However if we assume that workers learn from their past experiences of rising prices they will begin to base their behaviour on what they **ANTICIPATE** the rate of inflation to be and begin to bargain in **REAL** terms i.e. they see through the money illusion. Workers will only offer themselves for employment if they believe their **REAL WAGE** will rise. The greater the anticipated rate of inflation the greater the increase in **MONEY** wages workers will demand in order to maintain the value of their real wage.

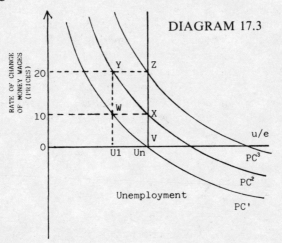

DIAGRAM 17.3

9. According to Friedman the long run Phillips Curve is **VERTICAL** at the **NATURAL RATE OF UNEMPLOYMENT** i.e. there is **NO** long run trade-off between inflation and unemployment. For each level of anticipated inflation there will be a different Phillips Curve. In diagram 17.3 the three curves indicated represent different expected inflation rates. Un represents the natural rate of unemployment. If the government believes this rate of unemployment to be too high and attempts to reduce it to U1 by expansionary fiscal and monetary policies the economy moves to point W with 10% inflation. This increase in the price level reduces real wages making labour more attractive so firms employ additional labour and expand output and then pass on the wage increase in the form of higher prices. The workers accepting employment did so because they believed their real wages had risen. At point W however

they realise that they have over estimated the increase in their real wage. As workers experience the 10% inflation rate they begin to anticipate inflation of 10% and the Phillips Curve shifts to the right to $PC^2$ which is consistent with 10% inflation. As workers are interested only in the **REAL WAGE** and this has now fallen due to inflation to what it was originally, unemployment returns to the natural rate at point X as workers leave those jobs where the real wage has not risen and search for jobs with a higher real wage. At point X inflation is 10% and unemployment has returned to Un. At X if the government wishes to reduce unemployment again to U1 by expanding demand it will result in a 20% inflation rate at point Y, and then shift to $PC^3$ as workers learn to anticipate a 20% inflation rate. Again the same process is followed with a return to the natural rate at Z, the same level of unemployment but with a 20% rate of inflation. There is therefore no long term trade-off, workers are temporarily 'fooled' into thinking their real wages have risen by governments pursuing expansionary policies, but unemployment returns to the natural rate accompanied by accelerating inflation. The 'actual' Phillips Curve is the vertical line V-Z. The implication being that in the long run that governments cannot permanently reduce unemployment below the natural rate by using fiscal and monetary policy, it can however have a choice of the rate of inflation, which will be stable at the natural rate. The incorporation of expectations into the analysis provides one explanation of the observed behaviour of the Phillips Curve.

10.    The way in which people formed their expectations in the previous analysis suggests that people's adjustments to rising prices takes time. This implies that they form their expectations about future prices by projecting their past experience of **ACTUAL** prices, with most weight being given to the most recent past, i.e. it is a model which contains a series of lagged responses with declining weights given to the responses as they are more distant in time. It is therefore referred to as the **ADAPTIVE EXPECTATIONS** model. This approach does allow for the possibility of demand management policies if the size of the lags could be estimated and appropriate weights selected, although Friedman would suggest that this possibility was unlikely because of the extreme variability of the lagged responses.

11.    The adaptive expectations model has been criticised by a number of economists on the grounds that if people operate on this

basis then they are going to be systematically in error which is clearly not rational. Putting it simply, people generally learn from their experiences so there is no reason to expect them not to in the labour market. The **RATIONAL EXPECTATIONS** model suggests that when people form views about the future they will take into account **ALL AVAILABLE INFORMATION**. If this is the case it has very important implications and suggests that demand management policies may be incapable of achieving their objectives. For example if the government attempts to reduce unemployment by expansionary fiscal and monetary policies people will anticipate the increase in prices and the effect of the budget deficit on future interest rates and taxes, and adjust their own consumption behaviour to accommodate them, thus neutralising the effects of government policy. The rational expectations model, if correct, would cast severe doubts upon the effectiveness of demand management policies.

## SELF ASSESSMENT QUESTIONS

1. Account for the apparent shift in the Phillips Curve which took place in the 1970's.

2. Why is 'money illusion' necessary for the operation of the orthodox Phillips Curve?

3. Outline the relationship between the natural rate of unemployment and inflation.

4. What is the rational expectations model and why does it cast doubt on the effectiveness of demand management policies?

# Chapter 18

# THE IS-LM MODEL

1.  The methods used to analyse national income, in particular the use of 45° lines and the aggregate demand curve, are subject to the criticism that they ignore the monetary and assets sector of the economy. The IS-LM model attempts to overcome this by incorporating both the **REAL** and **MONETARY** sectors. (This Chapter may be considered as optional by A level students but the model is becoming more widely used as a tool of analysis.)

2.  The IS function represents the **REAL** sector of the economy i.e. goods and services, and the **IS CURVE** indicates the combinations of **NATIONAL INCOME AND INTEREST RATES AT WHICH DESIRED INVESTMENT DEMAND IS EQUAL TO DESIRED SAVINGS**.

3.  The IS curve can be derived algebraically or geometrically. Diagram 18.1 illustrates the geometrical derivation using four quadrants. The analysis assumes all prices are constant, with a closed economy.

Diagram 18.1 consists of four quadrants which are read anti-clockwise, from 18.1(a) to 18.1(d).

3.1   Quadrant 18.1(a) relates the quantity of investment to the rate of interest and is therefore the demand curve for capital, or Marginal Efficiency of Capital curve (see Chapter 15).

3.2   In Quadrant 18.1(b) the 45° line represents the equilibrium condition for the closed economy, derived in Chapter 12, of **SAVING = INVESTMENT (S = I)**. The horizontal axis measures the amount of investment demand corresponding with that in 18.1(a) and the appropriate amount of savings for equilibrium can be identified by reading it off from the 45° line, as the 45° line will produce an equal reading on both axes.

3.3   Quadrant 18.1(c) incorporates the savings function derived in Chapter 12. Savings are assumed to be positively related to income so the savings function slopes upwards, the steepness of the slope being dependent upon the Marginal Propensity to Save. The

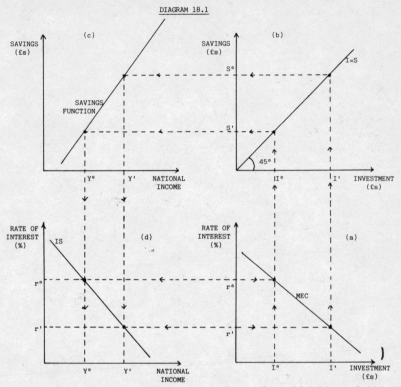

DIAGRAM 18.1

equilibrium quantity of savings is projected from 18.1(b) to 18.1(c) where the level of National Income necessary to generate the required level of saving for equilibrium can be established.

3.4    Quadrant 18.1(d) shows the derivation of the IS curve. The horizontal axis shows National Income and corresponds with that in quadrant 18.1(c)..Projecting down from 18.1(c) to 18.1(d) and where this coincides with the appropriate rate of interest from 18.1(a) produces one unique point on the IS curve where the combination of the rate of interest and national income will produce equality between desired saving and desired investment. By sequentially deriving numerous points such as A and B the IS curve can be derived.

4.

4.1    Government expenditure can easily be incorporated into the model by horizontally adding it to the M.E.C. curve in quadrant

18.1(a) and shifting the curve to the right, i.e. I + G.

4.2   In order to incorporate taxation a similar adjustment is made to the savings function in 18.1(c), where taxation shifts the curve to the left, i.e. S + T.

In neither case is the fundamental analysis altered, and the IS curve will be assumed here to incorporate both Government expenditure and taxation.

5.   The **STEEPNESS** of the **SLOPE** of the IS curve is determined by:

5.1   The **INTEREST ELASTICITY (SENSITIVITY)** of **INVESTMENT**. The more sensitive is investment to the rate of interest the **FLATTER** is the IS curve.

5.2   The **MARGINAL PROPENSITY TO SAVE** (MPS). The higher the MPS the steeper the IS curve.

6.   **SHIFTS** in the IS curve result from:

6.1   Changes in **GOVERNMENT EXPENDITURE**. An **INCREASE** in Government expenditure will shift the IS curve to the **RIGHT**, and a **REDUCTION** to the **LEFT**.

6.2   Changes in the **RATE OF INCOME TAX**. An **INCREASE** in tax will shift the curve to the **LEFT**, and a **REDUCTION** to the **RIGHT**.

7.   The IS curve **REPRESENTS THE REAL,** or **GOODS AND SERVICES SECTOR OF THE ECONOMY,** and as it represents equilibrium then the aggregate demand for goods and services will be equal to aggregate supply at all points on the curve.

8.   The **LM** curve represents the **MONETARY SECTOR** of the economy and can also be derived by utilising a four quadrant diagram. The derivation of the LM curve is illustrated in diagram 18.2.

8.1   Quadrant 18.2(a) indicates the **DEMAND FOR SPECULATIVE MONEY BALANCES** relative to the rate of interest. The resulting relationship is downward sloping representing the inverse relationship between asset prices (bonds) and the rate of interest (see Chapter 15).

8.2   Quadrant 18.2(b) is referred to as the **MONEY SUPPLY LINE**. Projecting upwards from 18.2(a) to 18.2(b) we obtain the size

DIAGRAM 18.2

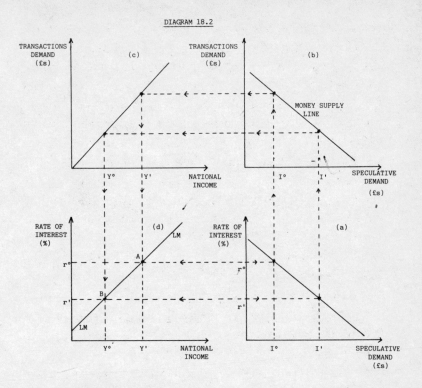

of speculative money balances, and if we assume that the only other significant money balances are **TRANSACTIONS BALANCES**, then given a fixed supply of money the difference must be the **TRANSACTIONS BALANCES** which can be identified on the vertical axis of 18.2(b). The greater the speculative balances the smaller are the transactions balances and vice versa and the sum of the two will be equal to the fixed money supply as the line intersects both axis at the same total value. It therefore indicates the distribution of the money supply between the two types of money balance, and given the level of speculative balances in 18.2(a) it indicates the level of demand for real transactions balances which is consistent with monetary equilibrium.

8.3   Projecting this level of transaction demand horizontally to quadrant 18.2(c) the level of National Income required to generate that level of transactions demand can be identified. The transactions demand function slopes upward with income as these balances will need to be larger as income rises in order to maintain the larger number of transactions.

8.4   Quadrant 18.2(d) has the rate of interest on the vertical axis and National Income on the horizontal axis. The level of National Income from 18.2(c) is projected down and where this coincides with the appropriate rate of interest a single point on the LM curve is identified. Starting with different interest rates and following the process around the quadrants produce numerous such points which can be connected to give the LM curve.

9.   The steepness of the **SLOPE** of the LM curve depends upon:

9.1   The **INTEREST ELASTICITY (SENSITIVITY)** of the speculative demand for money. The greater the interest elasticity the **FLATTER** the curve.

9.2   The sensitivity of the transactions demand for money to changes in National Income. The more sensitive the demand the **STEEPER** the LM curve.

10.   **SHIFTS** in the LM curve occur as a result of changes in the **SUPPLY OF MONEY**. An increase in the money supply shifting the LM curve to the right, and reductions shifting it to the left.

DIAGRAM 18.3

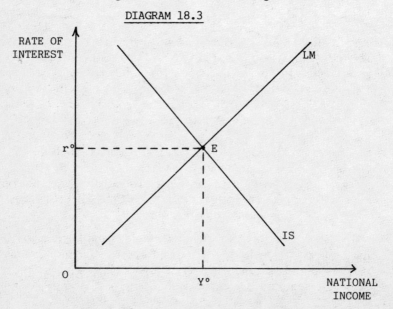

11. **EACH POINT ON THE LM CURVE INDICATES A RATE OF INTEREST AND LEVEL OF NATIONAL INCOME FOR WHICH THE TOTAL DEMAND FOR MONEY IS EQUAL TO THE TOTAL SUPPLY OF MONEY** and as such represents **EQUILIBRIUM IN THE MONETARY SECTOR.**

12. The complete IS-LM model combines both the IS and LM curves and the intersection of the two curves represents the combination of the rate of interest and National Income which **SIMULTANEOUSLY PRODUCES EQUILIBRIUM IN BOTH THE MONETARY AND REAL SECTORS OF THE ECONOMY AND THEREFORE THE ECONOMY AS A WHOLE.** This unique equilibrium point is illustrated in diagram 18.3, with interest rate $r°$ and national income $Y°$.

13. The IS-LM model can be used to illustrate the effects of either fiscal or monetary policy. An increase in Government expenditure will have the effect of shifting the IS curve to the right. This is illustrated in diagram 18.4.

DIAGRAM 18.4

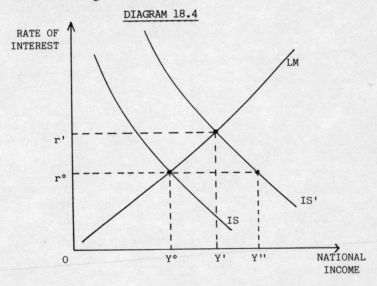

In diagram 18.4 the increase in government expenditure shifts the IS curve from IS to IS'. If we assume that the rate of interest **REMAINS CONSTANT** then income shifts from $Y°$ to $Y''$, this is the full multiplier effect discussed in Chapter 12. Incorporating the monetary effects of the increased expenditure indicates that the increase in income will be associated with an **INCREASE IN THE INTEREST RATE**, and income will rise only to Y' with an increase in the interest rate to r'. The rise in the interest rate '**CROWDS OUT**' some private expenditure and the increase in income is less than it would have been if the rate of interest had remained constant. The '**CROWDING OUT EFFECT**' therefore **REDUCES THE SIZE OF THE MULTIPLIER**. The rise in interest rates results from:

13.1    The need to offer higher rates of interest on government bonds in order to attract the public to buy them.

13.2    The increased demand for money as income rises.

14.    It is also necessary to consider the affect of the change in private **WEALTH** which may occur as a result of a budget deficit financed by the issue of government bonds.

14.1    A budget deficit will normally involve an increase in the holding of bonds by the public. This represents an increase in private **WEALTH**, which results in greater consumption out of any given income, in which case the **WEALTH EFFECT** augments the multiplier effect.

14.2    The increase in wealth however, will also have an affect on financial markets. It is argued by monetarists that where the government's deficit is financed by the issue of bonds there may be a further level of crowding out. This occurs as a result of the fall in bond prices which accompanies the rise in interest rates mentioned above. The fall in bond prices reduces the wealth of bond holders who then increase the level of their savings in order to regain their previous levels of wealth, this **WEALTH EFFECT** further reduces private expenditures and dampens the multiplier effect.

14.3    Whether the net result of these two influences is expansionary or contractionary will depend upon their relative strengths.

15.    The debate over the advocacy of monetary policy (monetarists) relative to fiscal policy (generally Keynesians) can be analysed by utilising IS-LM curve analysis and making different assumptions about the relative slopes of the curves.

**15.1 MONETARISTS ASSUME THAT THE DEMAND FOR MONEY HAS ZERO INTEREST ELASTICITY** i.e. is inelastic, the LM curve is therefore very steep, or vertical. Investment is assumed to be interest elastic and the IS curve therefore has a shallower slope. In diagram 18.5 an increase in Government spending shifts the IS curve to IS' but due to the inelastic money demand income remains unchanged at $\overline{Y}$ and the impact falls upon the rate of interest which rises to r'. **FISCAL POLICY IS THEREFORE INEFFECTIVE.** Alternatively **INCREASING THE MONEY SUPPLY** as illustrated in diagram 18.6 shifts the LM curve to the right and has a **POWERFUL EFFECT UPON INCOME.**

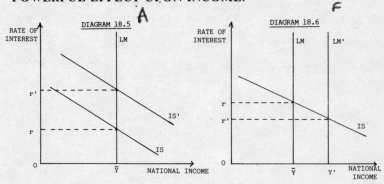

**15.2 KEYNESIANS** assume that the **DEMAND FOR MONEY IS INTEREST ELASTIC** (see Chapter 15) and the LM curve therefore has a shallower slope. Interest rates are assumed to have little effect upon investment demand which implies that the IS curve is steeper. The relative slopes are illustrated in diagram 18.7 and 18.8.

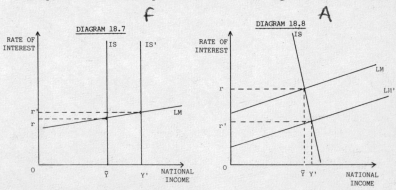

In diagram 18.7 an increase in government expenditure shifts the IS curve to IS' increasing income from $\overline{Y}$ to Y', **FISCAL POLICY THEREFORE HAS A POWERFUL EFFECT UPON INCOME.** Diagram 18.8 illustrates an increase in the money supply which shifts the LM curve from LM to LM' leaving income only slightly changed at Y', the impact falling upon interest rates. **MONETARY POLICY IS THEREFORE AN INEFFECTIVE POLICY INSTRUMENT** for generating changes in income.

15.3  In the extreme case, which Keynes referred to as the **LIQUIDITY TRAP,** the demand for money becomes **INFINITELY ELASTIC** and all increases in the money supply are held in the form of speculative money balances. This is represented by the horizontal portion of the LM curve, A-B, in diagram 18.9. In the liquidity trap monetary policy would be totally ineffective, and changes in income could only be brought about through the use of **FISCAL POLICY.**

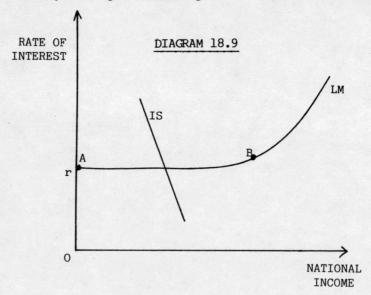

16.  The interest elasticity of the demand for money is an empirical matter and there appears to be little evidence to support the extreme cases. In the 'normal' case illustrated in diagram 18.3 both fiscal and monetary policy have a role to play.

## SELF ASSESSMENT QUESTIONS

1.  What does the IS curve represent?

2.  What does the LM curve represent?

3.  What is represented by the intersection of the IS and LM curve?

4.  Explain the difference between the monetarist and Keynesian viewpoint by utilising IS-LM curves.

5.  Under what circumstances would monetary policy be totally ineffective?

# Chapter 19
# TRADE UNIONS

1.  The economic theory of wage determination is discussed in the companion volume to this text entitled Basic Concepts in Micro Economics, however it is impossible in an industrial society to analyse the factors which determine wages without giving some consideration to the role and influence of TRADE UNIONS.

2.  Although we are mainly concerned here with the affect of Trade Unions on wages it is important to be aware of the wider role of Trade Unions. The Donovan Report (1968) considered the role of Trade Unions under three main headings:

2.1 Promoting the interests of their members.
2.2 Accelerating the economic advance of the nation.
2.3 Accelerating the social advance of the nation.

3.  Wage rates and conditiòns are determined by the process referred to as COLLECTIVE BARGAINING, whereby the union officials bargain with employers on behalf of their members. Collective bargaining generally occurs at the national level and the pay rates determined apply to a whole industry and are embodied

### TABLE 19.1

| Year | Men | Women (Millions) | Total | Total Membership as a % of Total Employees (%) |
|------|-----|------------------|-------|-----------------------------------------------|
| 1951 | 7.7 | 1.8 | 9.5  | 45 |
| 1961 | 7.9 | 2.0 | 9.9  | 43 |
| 1971 | 8.4 | 2.8 | 11.1 | 49 |
| 1976 | 8.8 | 3.6 | 12.4 | 52 |
| 1977 | 9.1 | 3.8 | 12.8 | 53 |
| 1978 | 9.2 | 3.9 | 13.1 | 54 |
| 1979 | 9.4 | 3.9 | 13.3 | 55 |
| 1980 | 9.2 | 3.8 | 12.9 | 53 |
| 1981 | 8.4 | 3.8 | 12.1 | 50 |
| 1982 |     |     | 11.6 | 48 |

Source: Social Trends 1985

within a national agreement. This agreement may be supplemented
by additional payments or benefits negotiated locally at plant level.
Nationwide collective bargaining has the advantage for both unions
and management of reducing the costs of bargaining below what it
would be if employers and employees negotiated individually.

4.   Trade Union membership in the UK grew throughout the 20th
century, but with the main periods of growth being around the two
World Wars, the late 1960's and the 1970's; but with membership
declining in the 1980's as a consequence of rising unemployment.
Table 19.1 indicates the pattern of Trade Union membership in the
UK.

5.   It is often argued that unions can raise their members' wage rates
only at the cost of reducing the number employed. Such analysis
assumes that the demand for labour is competitive and the demand
curve is static. In diagram 19.1, DD is the demand curve for labour

DIAGRAM 19.1

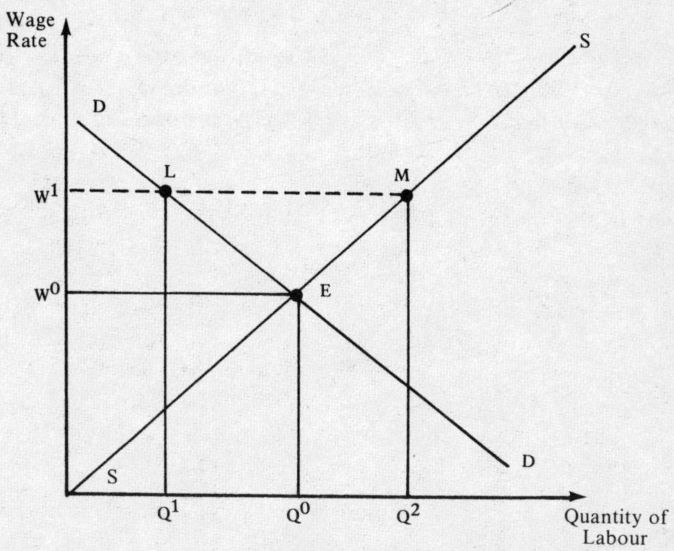

and SS the supply curve. The equilibrium wage is $W^0$ with $Q^0$ labour
employed. If the union now enforces a wage increase to $W^1$ which is
the minimum wage at which union members are allowed to work, the
demand for labour falls to $Q^1$ (L) as a consequence of:

5.1 The higher price being charged for the product being produced, which is necessary to cover the wage rise.

5.2 Factor substitution as capital is substituted for labour in the production process as it is now relatively cheaper.

The supply curve for labour is now $W^1$ M S with no labour supplied below the minimum wage ($W^1$) and an infinite amount up to M ($Q^2$), the labour supply curve is therefore infinitely elastic along the portion $W^1$ L M, but the labour supply will not increase above M ($Q^2$) without a higher wage rate. The new supply curve intersects the original demand curve at L, the new equilibrium point, with $Q^1$ labour demanded, whilst the quantity supplied at that wage rate is $Q^2$. The quantity of labour employed has been reduced by $Q^0 - Q^1$ and there is an excess labour supply of $Q^1 - Q^2$ (L—M) at the prevailing wage rate. This type of analysis however ignores changes in productivity and Chapter 15 in Micro Economics shows how an **INCREASE IN THE MARGINAL PRODUCTIVITY OF LABOUR CAN MAINTAIN THE NUMBERS EMPLOYED.** Such increases in marginal productivity can be achieved through the adoption of new technology and more efficient working practices.

6. The extent to which a union can influence wages in a particular industry also depends upon the elasticity of demand for labour. This is discussed in detail in Basic Concepts in Micro Economics. Generally it is the case that the more inelastic the demand for labour the greater the scope a union will have for gaining a wage increase for its members. In any particular occupation the scope for gaining wage increases will also be influenced by supply factors, the more inelastic the supply the greater the scope for maintaining, or obtaining, high wage rates. Unions therefore have an incentive to restrict the supply of labour to any particular occupation by imposing entry conditions such as lengthy apprenticeships. Where there are few restrictions upon entry to an occupation, ie. unskilled occupations, the union may need to substitute the threat of withdrawal of labour as a means of influencing wages.

7. The extent to which unions can raise the wage rates of their members may also depend upon a number of other factors such as the attitudes of the membership, the degree of geographical concentration, the stability of employment, and the degree of competition amongst employers. Studies indicate that the hourly pay rate in an industry where the labour force is unionised and covered by

a collective bargaining agreement will be 8—10% higher than in a similar non-unionised industry.

8. Trade Unions, and relative demand elasticities are important factors in explaining the pay differentials which exist between occupations, a particularly important source of higher earnings being the length of training and level of education required. Adam Smith referred to **EQUALIZING** and **NON-EQUALIZING DIFFERENTIALS** and suggested that in a competitive labour market the **NET ADVANTAGES** of an occupation would **TEND TO EQUALITY.** Equalising advantages were factors such as unpleasantness, dirt and discomfort, non-equalizing differentials were wages. In an unpleasant occupation there would be higher wages to compensate and in pleasant occupations wages would be lower, and over a lifetime the net advantages between occupations will be equalized. In reality it is frequently the lowest paid occupations which are also the most unpleasant, as they are generally unskilled and entry to them is easy and those in such occupations have no alternative available to them.

9. Wages may also differ between people in the same occupations. One reason may be differentials as a reward for experience or length of service, or where pay scales are structured according to age. A major source of wage differentials is sex, as women even within the same occupation are frequently paid less than men. Women also tend to be concentrated into the occupations with the lowest rates of pay, such as catering and hairdressing. The combination of these two factors means that on average women earn considerably less than men, and studies suggest that women's earnings are approximately 75% of men's despite the Equal Pay Act 1975. The main reasons suggested for this apparent discrimination against women are:

9.1 Their weaker attachment to the labour force due to the convention that they look after children, and the need to be absent from work when having children.

9.2 Absenteeism and labour turnover is higher for women than it is for men.

9.3 As a consequence of the weaker attachment to the labour force women gain less experience and seniority in the work-place, and employers are less willing therefore to give training to women, which reduces their value in the workforce.

9.4 Women tend to be concentrated in industries which consist of numerous small-scale establishments in which national wage rates tend to be lower than in the larger more concentrated industries. These also tend to be industries in which a lower proportion of the workforce belongs to Trade Unions due to the high costs of organising.

10. Even within the same occupational group women tend to earn less than men, for example, within primary school teaching women earn 13% less than men, although the main source of this differential is not that women are paid less for the same job but that fewer of them occupy the higher paid teaching positions, due probably to the reasons given above. If it is also considered that females work predominately part-time, (40% of total females in work compared to 5% for males) then the disparity· in wages becomes even more pronounced. The anomaly of low pay for women has been only marginally influenced by Equal Pay legislation, although it may be too soon to judge the combined affect of this legislation together with the Sex Discrimination Act 1975 and the Employment Protection Act 1976. If however, for the reasons given above, it is not discrimination but a reflection of a lower marginal revenue product which results in lower female wages then it may also be necessary to raise the marginal productivity of women by giving them more incentive to remain in the workforce; for example, better career prospects, training and a more appropriate educational structure.

## SELF ASSESSMENT QUESTIONS

1. What is meant by 'collective bargaining'?

2. Under what circumstances can a Trade Union simultaneously raise wages and maintain employment?

3. Explain the differences in wage rates both between occupations and between males and females.

4. What is meant by equalizing and non-equalizing differentials?

# Chapter 20
# POPULATION

1. Population refers to the number of people living in a particular area. In the study of population however, it is not only the absolute number of people which is of interest, but also the rate of change of the population size and also its composition. The study of population is important because of its economic implications, in particular the way in which change in the population can affect changes in the demand for goods and services, and therefore the allocation of society's resources.

2. The total population of the UK, and the rest of the world, was characterised by a rapid growth throughout the 19th Century and this growth has continued in the rest of the world throughout the 20th Century, although in the UK since 1971 the total has remained fairly level with only slow growth projected to the end of the century. Table 20.1 shows the population growth for the UK. The size of the UK population is found from a census which has been held every 10 years since 1801.

```
                      TABLE 20.1
                 UK POPULATION (MILLIONS)

        1851                22.3
        1901                38.2
        1921                44.0
        1931                46.0
        1951                50.2
        1961                52.7
        1971                55.5
        1981                56.3
        1983                56.3    (Estimated)
        2003                56.1    (Forecast)
        Source 1. Registrar General.
```

3. Although it is important to know the size of the **TOTAL POPULATION** it is also important to have details of the **COMPOSITION OF THE POPULATION,** in particular an estimate is required of the following.

3.1 **WORKING POPULATION** — the proportion of the population in the working age group 16—65 (60 for females).

3.2 **AGE/SEX STRUCTURE** — Age structure refers to the number of persons in each of three groupings.
  (i)   Young persons — below 16.
  (ii)  Working age groups, 16—65 (60 for females).
  (iii) Men over 65 and women over 60.

Age/sex distribution refers to the number of males and females in each age grouping.

4. Both Total Population and the population structure have important implications for the nation's standard of living. Income per head or **PER CAPITA INCOME** for a nation is calculated as:

$$\text{PER CAPITA INCOME} = \frac{\text{NATIONAL INCOME}}{\text{POPULATION}}$$

From this equation it can be seen that even if national income is growing per capita income may fall if the rate of growth of national income is exceeded by the rate of growth of population, and it is this problem which faces many 'Third World' countries.

5. Changes in the composition of the population alters the balance between producers and consumers over time. As stated above the age group 16—65 form the working population whilst those in the 0—16 and 65+ groups can be regarded as the dependent population. An increase in the size of the dependent population relative to the working population, referred to as the **DEPENDENCY RATIO,** means that living standards would fall unless there is an increase in the real output of the working population as a result of increased productivity, for example; by the adoption of new technology. Changes in the composition of the population also affects the demand for **AGE RELATED GOODS AND SERVICES,** and for this reason has important implications for firms, local authorities and central government. An increase in the number of people in the 65+ age group, referred to as an **AGEING POPULATION,** increases the demand for social provision for the aged, appropriate medical provision, and increases the burden of pensions on the working population. Although the UK population remained fairly level between 1971 and 1983 the proportion aged less than 15 fell and the proportion over 65 increased. Population projections up to 2001

show a rise in the numbers over 65 with the most significant increase in those over 85. Within the older age group females predominate as their life expectancy exceeds that of males. In 1983 women outnumbered men in the age group of 50 upwards, and in the 75 or over age group the ratio of women to men was 2 to 1. Both females and males today however have a 50% chance of achieving a life expectancy of 70 years. This increase in life expectancy has been the result of the improvement in living standards, medical advances, and the extension of welfare services for the older age groups.

6.   The age/sex distribution of the population can be illustrated by the use of **POPULATION PYRAMIDS** as illustrated.

DIAGRAM 20.1

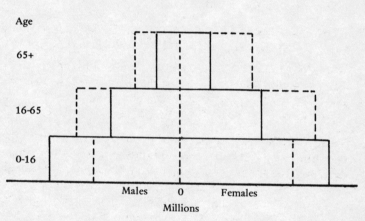

The population pyramid illustrates the age/sex distribution of the population, the dotted lines showing the affect of an ageing population on the shape of the population pyramid.

7.   Births and deaths are usually expressed as **CRUDE BIRTH** and **DEATH RATES.** These are calculated as the number of births/deaths per 1000 population.

ie.   **NUMBER OF BIRTHS x 1000**

**TOTAL POPULATION**

7.1  The **CRUDE BIRTH RATE** is influenced by factors such as the state of medical knowledge, social and economic factors, social mores such as the attitudes towards family size, contraception, and religion.

7.2 The **CRUDE DEATH RATE** is influenced by social and economic conditions, medical knowledge, hygiene and living standards, and the infant mortality rate (ie. the deaths of children below 1 year of age).

8.  The improvement in the average life expectancy in the UK to 70 years has been the result of the advances in medical care and the extension of welfare services for the elderly and in addition the affect of the general rise in living standards. The most significant fall in the death rate has resulted from lower infant mortality which has been a consequence of improved medical facilities, improvements in diet and housing, and the improvements in ante and post natal care.

9.  The overall size of the population is determined by the **NATURAL INCREASE**, ie. **BIRTHS** minus **DEATHS**. In the UK during the 20th Century the change in the birth rate is seen as being the major influence on population size as the death rate has remained fairly constant. The birth rate, despite its falling trend, is more liable to sudden variations. Unexpected increases in the birth rate, or 'baby booms', create **POPULATION BULGES** such as those which occurred after the two World Wars and in the mid-1960's. Such bulges then pass through the population structure over time creating an increased demand for age related goods and services which may not be required in such quantities when the bulge in the population has passed. For example the 'baby booms' of the mid-1960's increased the demand for schools, but as the bulge passes into the older age group the demand for schooling falls resulting in falling school rolls and surplus school capacity. In the 21st Century there will be an increase in the demand for pensions as the population bulge moves into the pensionable age group.

10.   The major changes in population are of three types:

10.1 **BIRTH RATE EXCEEDING DEATH RATE** resulting in an **INCREASING POPULATION.**

10.2 **DEATH RATE EXCEEDING BIRTH RATE** resulting in a **DECREASING POPULATION.**

10.3 **EXCEPTIONAL INCREASES** in the Birth Rate resulting in a **POPULATION BULGE.**

NET MIGRATION which is calculated as IMMIGRATION MINUS EMIGRATION has not seriously affected the UK population over the long term. Net migration is more likely to affect the quality of the working population, particularly if the most talented, healthiest, or skilled members of the workforce choose to emmigrate.

11. The concept of the OPTIMUM POPULATION is central to the study of the economics of population. OPTIMUM POPULATION CAN BE DEFINED AS THE POPULATION SIZE WHICH MAXIMISES THE OUTPUT (PER HEAD) OF THE ECONOMY. The concept of optimum population assumes that technology, trade and competition remains constant and only the population size varies. Given these assumptions, then as the population size increases output will initially increase, but eventually DIMINISHING RETURNS set in and as population grows further output per head declines. This is illustrated in Diagram 20.2. Output per head is maximised at X with population OM.

DIAGRAM 20.2

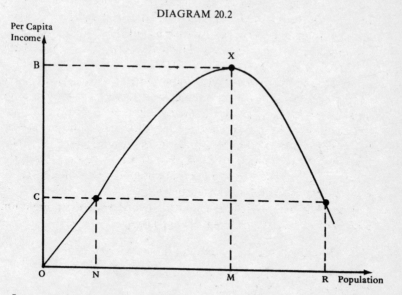

Increases in population above OM cause output per head to fall and M—R can therefore be referred to as OVER-POPULATED, with population OR giving a lower per capital income (OC) than population OM. Population ON fails to exploit the returns to scale and therefore also has a lower per capita income than OM; also having per capita income OC. NM can therefore be referred to as being **UNDER-POPULATED**.

12. If the assumption that technology is fixed is dropped however, it may be possible for increased **PRODUCTIVITY THROUGH TECHNOLOGICAL CHANGE TO OFFSET THE EFFECT OF DIMINISHING RETURNS** and the optimum population may coincide with the actual population as population grows. In diagram 20.3 as population grows from OM to OT technological change increases productivity per head offsetting the effect of diminishing returns shifting the most efficient, or optimum, point from X to S; the optimum population being the same as the actual population OT.

DIAGRAM 20.3

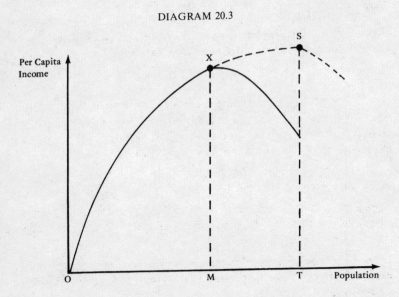

As population growth takes place there could be a succession of points such as X and S each giving a higher per capita income and therefore standard of living.

13. One of the earliest discussions of population size was that by the **REV. THOMAS MALTHUS** in his essay "The Principle of Population as it affects the future improvement of Society" (1798), which was refined in a second essay in 1803. Mathus examined the relationship between **POPULATION SIZE** and the **MEANS OF**

SUBSISTENCE; in particular the production of food. Malthus postulated that any increase in living standards would result in an increase in population size, however **FOOD PRODUCTION COULD NOT INCREASE AT THE SAME RATE AS POPULATION GROWTH. POPULATION GROWTH WOULD THEREFORE ALWAYS EXCEED THE GROWTH OF THE MEANS OF SUBSISTENCE** and mankind was doomed to remain in poverty living at the subsistence level. According to Malthus the population was kept within its means of subsistence by the 'misery' of famine, war, disease, and pestilence. The only escape for civilisation from this vicious circle of poverty was through what Malthus referred to as 'moral restraint' by which he meant later marriage and therefore fewer children — a solution Malthus himself thought was unlikely.

14. Malthus' gloomy predictions proved to be incorrect — the population during the 19th Century grew rapidly and so too did living standards. The weaknesses in Malthus's argument were as follows:

14.1 The Malthusian argument is essentially one of diminishing returns with land as a fixed factor. In fact land was not a fixed factor as new food growing areas were developed overseas and food was imported, eg. Wheat from the American Prairies.

14.2 Malthus did not foresee the rate of technological change which enabled living standards to rise alongside population growth.

14.3 Improvements in methods of birth control and their general acceptance within society, and changed social attitudes towards family size.

14.4 Malthus considered people only as consumers but generally each consumer is also a producer, therefore a larger population creates a greater output.

15. The Malthusian doctrine can therefore be considered as a special case of the Law of Diminishing Returns, the affects of which were offset in Britain by changes in other factors as listed above. The lessons of Malthus cannot however be totally ignored as it will always be necessary to relate finite resources to the demands of society and in many 'Third World' countries where populations are growing more rapidly than the means of subsidence the principles advocated by Malthus are still relevant today.

## SELF ASSESSMENT QUESTIONS

1. What are the main causes of changes in the population size?

2. What is meant by the term 'Optimum Population'?

3. How does a change in the population structure affect the demand for goods and services?

4. What did Malthus predict about the future of mankind and why was he proved wrong?

# Chapter 21
# ECONOMIC GROWTH & DEVELOPMENT

1. Economic growth refers to the increase in the economy's productive capacity. It is usual to express this in terms of the growth of Gross Domestic Product (GDP).

2. Care must be taken in comparing GDP figures over time and making assumption regarding economic growth from them for three reasons:

2.1 Comparisons must take account of inflation and therefore can only be made in 'deflated' data, i.e. data at constant prices.

2.2 An increase in GDP from a position of unemployed resources and deficient demand to one of full employment does not constitute economic growth as there has been no growth in productive potential. When comparisons between different time periods are made it is important therefore that the level of resource utilisation is similar.

2.3 Even when GDP is growing, living standards may decline if the population growth is more rapid (see Chapter 1). **Per capita GDP** is the relevant measure and is calculated as:

$$\frac{GDP}{Population}$$

3. Economic growth is generally considered to be desirable by governments because it brings in its train other benefits which are seen as being desirable. Increased GDP implies higher incomes and therefore a higher standard of living in terms of material goods. Higher incomes also imply higher tax revenues for the government which should facilitate an improved level of provision of public services such as education, health, and other social services. The greater the rate of economic growth the more rapid the increase in living standards, as conventionally defined, will be.

4. The main cause of concern for the British economy has not been just the slow rate of growth which has been apparent but the fact that the growth rate has been slow relative to other industrial countries.

Table 21.1 indicates the U.K.'s growth rate from 1950 to 1980 and Table 21.2 the U.K.'s growth rate for 1970 to 1980 relative to a selection of other industrialised countries.

| TABLE 21.1 | |
|---|---|
| U.K. | GDP percentage increase per annum |
| 1950-1960 | 2.5 |
| 1960-1970 | 2.7 |
| 1970-1980 | 1.9 |

Source: O.E.C.D.

| TABLE 21.2 | |
|---|---|
| | GDP Annual percentage increase 1970-1980 |
| FRANCE | 3.9 |
| GERMANY | 2.9 |
| JAPAN | 5.4 |
| NORWAY | 4.4 |
| U.K. | 2.2 |
| CANADA | 4.4 |
| U.S.A. | 2.4 |

Source: O.E.C.D.

Britain's relatively poor performance is even more pronounced when considered over the longer time period. Japan sustained a growth in real per capita GDP of 7.3% per annum between 1950 and 1978, France 3.8%, West Germany 4.5%, whilst over the same period per capita GDP in the U.K. grew by only 2.1%.

5.  In order to establish why growth rates differ it is necessary to identify the sources of economic growth. Economic growth is generated by an increase in both the **QUALITY** and **QUANTITY** of the nation's productive resources, in particular labour and capital.

### 5.1 LABOUR

(i)  **THE QUANTITY** or **SUPPLY** of labour depends upon trends in the growth of working population, hours worked, the length of holidays and net migration.

(ii)  The **QUALITY** of labour is determined by the resources and facilities available for training and education. Not only is the level of provision important but also the extent to which the skills being taught are appropriate to the needs of the economy as technological change takes place. The extent to which the labour force is willing to adapt to changes in technology and adopt new working practices is also an important factor. Investment in **HUMAN CAPITAL** has been identified as one of the major factors in generating economic growth.

### 5.2 CAPITAL

(i)   The size of the nation's stock of capital is an important factor in determining labour productivity. The more capital which is available per worker the greater will be labour productivity, referred to as the **CAPITAL:LABOUR** ratio. The larger the proportion of GNP which a nation devotes to **INVESTMENT** the greater will be the stock of capital. This **GROSS CAPITAL FORMATION** is a major determinant of economic growth, however the precise stock of capital at any point in time is difficult to calculate due to the unreliability of the estimates of depreciation. Increasing the amount of capital per unit of labour is referred to as **CAPITAL DEEPENING** whilst increasing the capital stock to keep abreast of increases in the size of the working population is referred to as **CAPITAL WIDENING. GROSS INVESTMENT** refers to **NEW INVESTMENT PLUS REPLACEMENT INVESTMENT** whilst **NET INVESTMENT** refers to **NEW INVESTMENT** only . It is therefore possible to have gross investment without net investment.

(ii)   The **QUALITY** of the capital stock is of major importance, and in particular the extent to which it embodies the most recent technology, an element which is difficult to quantify but is of major importance in generating growth. The assumption is that the most recent machines incorporate the recent scientific and technical developments and are therefore more productive than older machines. This view suggests that Gross Investment is the most important figure even if most of it is replacement investment as this reduces the average age of the capital stock and therefore increases its quality and efficiency. The example of countries such as Germany and Japan is frequently quoted in support of this argument. These countries lost most of their productive capacity during the Second World War and replaced their capital stock with new equipment containing more recent technology which enabled them to make more rapid growth than countries such as Britain where the average age of the capital stock was much greater. This is sometimes referred to as the 'catching up' theory. Productivity gains due to improvements in the quality, rather than the quantity, of capital are said to result from **EMBODIED TECHNICAL CHANGE.**

6.   For the reasons stated above the prospect of economic growth is attractive to governments and various measures have been adopted in the U.K. in the hope of achieving higher rates of growth. In planned economies it is less difficult to achieve a diversion of resources away from current consumption to investment and capital accumulation for future growth, but in a mixed economy with an electorate to appeal to resort has to be made to less direct means of stimulating growth. Measures which governments can utilise include:

6.1   Improvements in labour quality by increasing the provision of education, and training of an appropriate type, in particular youth training.

6.2   Use of the tax system in order to encourage investment, including allowances against tax for investment and depreciation. Differential rates of Corporation Tax on retained profits and dividends have also been used in the hope that lower rates on retentions would encourage a higher level of retentions and thereby increase investment (the extent to which such a policy is successful is however controversial).

6.3   Keeping interest rates low and allowing tax relief on interest in order to reduce the cost of borrowing and improve the viability of investment projects.

6.4   The encouragement of research and development by providing facilities and grants, and dispensing information from government sponsored research.

6.5   Encouraging the acceptance of new working practices and new technology into industry by discussion with employer groups, trade unions and government sponsored bodies.

6.6   The use of public sector investment as a source of growth. In particular capital spending on projects such as railway electrification and motorway construction.

7.   Governments have not however been particulary successful at improving growth rates. This is due largely to the problem of quantifying the relationship between the variables which are thought to influence growth and the amount of growth which changes in these variables actually generates. A further problem is that in a mixed economy too much intervention by government in order to achieve

the growth objective may appear as a move towards central planning, hence the preference for indirect incentives. Britain's only attempt at planning for growth, in the form of the National Plan 1965, attempted to stimulate growth by announcing a target growth rate of 4% per annum for 1964-1970, but was abandoned during its first year when an actual growth rate of only 2.4% was achieved. Failure was largely due to the problem discussed in Chapter 13 of achieving growth, balance of payments equilibrium, and price stability, simultaneously.

8.   It is by no means generally accepted that economic growth is beneficial to society and critics point to the following costs of economic growth:

8.1   Deterioration of the environment through urban sprawl and industrialisation.

8.2   The growth of environmental pollution to the atmosphere and rivers etc.

8.3   High rates of innovation making skills redundant and forcing unwanted change or obsolescence onto people.

8.4   The faster 'lifestyle' engendered by growth may bring in its wake illness and a reduced 'quality of life' e.g. heart attacks, ulcers, higher crime rates and suicide rates; which are all characteristic of urban industrialised societies.

8.5   It may be argued that higher levels of consumerism are not necessarily synonymous with a better 'quality of life' and as quickly as 'wants' are satisfied then new wants can be created by the large corporations utilising skilful advertising. Constantly attempting to strive to new levels of 'satisfaction' can itself be a cause of stress in individuals.

9.   Although in the advanced economies of the Western world economic growth for its own sake has been the subject of criticism, for many areas of the world the achievement of economic growth is of overridding concern. The under-developed countries in the south, or 'Third World' are not sufficiently developed to generate the necessary domestic savings required to finance investment for growth, and by implication industrialisation.

10.   These countries are usually characterised by some, or all, of the following:

10.1 Low income per head of population.

10.2 Rapidly growing populations.

10.3 Low capital investment per head of population.

10.4 Low volume of 'social' capital i.e. roads, schools, railways etc.

10.5 Low standards of education for the general population.

10.6 A reluctance to accept the 'materialistic' conventions of economically advanced countries.

10.7 Under-utilisation of natural resources.

10.8 Concentration on the production of primary agricultural products which bring little revenue due to their low and fluctuating prices on world markets.

11. The preamble to United Nations (U.N.) statistics on assistance given to developing nations defines the under-developed economies as:

11.1 All countries and territories in Africa with the exception of South Africa.

11.2 All countries and territories in America with the exception of the U.S.A and the U.S.A. Virgin Islands, Canada, Greenland, and Puerto Rico.

11.3 Asia with the exception of China, Democratic People's Republic of Korea, Vietnam, Japan, Mongolia and Turkey.

11.4 Oceania with the exception of Australia, New Zealand and U.S. possessions.

From this definition most of the world's population is placed in the category of 'the under-developed South'.

12. The reason that growth is seen as a desirable goal for these countries is that it should enable them to support their growing populations by producing sufficient food, goods or services to be able to engage in trade on world markets to earn the necessary foreign currency which would enable them to raise living standards.

13. Apart from the obvious moral obligations the developed countries have towards the 'Third World' countries there are sound economic reasons for encouraging growth:

13.1 If the developed economies could expand their trading base then according to the Law of Comparative Advantage greater specialisation could take place raising world output to the advantage of all concerned.

13.2 Political stability should be achieved as various governments will no longer hold the purse strings through the patronage of aid. Once growth is achieved and has matured into industrialisation enabling the country to stand on its own feet they would be independent of the influence of other governments.

14. There are however a number of **BARRIERS TO GROWTH**:

14.1 The rapid growth of population means that even if the economy is growing in terms of national income, if population growth is faster than the growth of national income then per capita incomes will be falling. The sort of situation described by Thomas Malthus in the 18th century.

14.2 The escalation of oil prices in the 1970's has forced the developing countries to devote a greater part of their national income to obtaining it. For many countries this has increased their national debt. In 1981 the IMF reported that interest payments on debts had almost doubled between 1978 and 1980.

14.3 Where developing countries have natural resources there may be limits to their utilisation owing to insufficient financial capital, lack of 'social' overhead capital or a deficiency in the capacity of human capital due to debilitating sicknesses such as malaria, bilharzia and cholera.

14.4 There is also the problem of inefficient use of resources. Inefficiency in this context derives from two sources:

(i) **ALLOCATIVE INEFFICIENCY** i.e. investment in the wrong products.

(ii) **'X' INEFFICIENCY** i.e. where investment is in the right product but is sub optimal owing to inadequate education, poor health, religion, customs and taboos.

14.5 The accumulation of capital requires that some current consumption be foregone. This becomes virtually impossible where living standards are already at a level where even survival is difficult. For this reason developing countries are forced to use borrowed capital, which is frequently tied to specific projects. The problem with this method of capital accumulation is the future commitment to meeting the debt, plus interest payments. An additional problem is that in the past loans have been given for inappropriate purposes, for example prestige investments which require a level of technological sophistication which is beyond the capacity of the recipient nation (elaborate hydro-electric schemes etc.).

15.   There are two approaches which are advocated for solving the problems of the developing countries, a free market 'trade' approach or a planned 'aid' approach.

15.1   Supporters of the free market 'trade' approach put the following points against the use of aid:

(i)   Aid diminishes the capacity for self help as it removes incentives to work and innovate, and is demoralising and undignified in that it puts the recipients into the position of a beggar.

(ii)   Aid is not given to the deserving poor but to their government and there is no guarantee that it will ever benefit the poor and may be used to maintain inefficient, uncaring and non representative governments in power.

(iii)   Aid may build up resentment in the donor countries, particularly during periods of recession.

(iv)   Investment decisions will not necessarily be made upon sound commercial grounds but by government planners who may opt for more prestigious but less essential projects.

(v)   Aid has so far made little impact on the problem.

15.2   Proponents of free trade as a solution suggest that commercial loans should be given in preference to aid. The industries which are able to attract commercial loans will generally be those which offer the best prospects of high returns and therefore the efficient use of resources. These industries will tend to be the industries which offer the best prospects for generating economic growth. In addition the supporters of the trade solution make the following points in support of the market approach:

(i)   Trade encourages specialisation according to the Laws of Comparative Advantage which is more efficient in the long run.

(ii)   Investment will be made on the grounds of commercial viability and will therefore be more efficient.

(iii) 'Self-help' creates greater incentives to work and innovate and is more dignified than aid.

15.3   The present development gap is however the result of over 150 years of the operation of such market forces and effects of free trade, where the benefits accrue to those strong enough to grab them since the initial starting point of the two parties will determine who gets what, and the market solution does not indicate how this gap can be closed.

16.   The foundations for modern aid were laid with the creation of the International Monetary Fund (IMF). Part of the IMF was the International Bank for Reconstruction and Development (IBRD), known as the 'World Bank' which was originally set up to assist the war damaged economies of Europe but since the 1950's has directed most of its funds to Third World governments for their national development plans. In 1964 a group of 77 developing nations formed a group to press the common interests of the Third World. The group, known as the United Nations Conference on Trade and Development (UNCTAD) has convened on five occasions in order to promote Third World interests, the most recent, UNCTAD 5, met in 1979 at Arusha, Tanzania, and emphasised a need for collective self reliance through South-South co-operation. In 1981 the Brandt Report stressed the importance of increased North-South co-operation in order to jolt the world economy out of recession. The main themes of the Brandt Report were: the stabilisation of Third World commodity prices as remunerative levels, the loosening of the rich industrial countries' grip on processing and marketing, the removal of tariff and other barriers to Third World manufactured goods and wider trade concessions. On the financial front the report suggested that Third World countries should have more say in the IMF and World Bank and that conditions attached to IMF loans should be less stringent and new Special Drawing Rights (SDR's) should go the South. The developed countries should increase aid to 0.7% GNP by 1985 and a World Development Fund should be established financed by international taxes on trade, arms sales and seabed exploration, which should be democratically controlled by the member governments. On the question of debt the report stated that 'massive resource transfers' should be made from the North in order to enable the South to maintain the interest payments on their debts and that more debts should be written off (e.g. as Britain has

done in the case of Uganda's £22 million). It also suggested that more loans as opposed to grants should be given and these loans should not be tied to particular projects. The report covered many other areas including agrarian reform, food distribution, mineral exploration and the proliferation of nuclear weapons. There has however been little evidence of firm action on the points raised by the Brandt Report, in particular on issues such as additional SDR's, largely due to the fear of stimulating world inflation and the fact that governments, in particular the U.S., who are cutting their domestic budgets, are unwilling to voice support for such measures.

17.  The problem of the developing nations presents the greatest challenge to economics but may in the long run offer the greatest prospect for the growth of world output and living standards.


## SELF ASSESSMENT QUESTIONS

1.  Define economic growth.

2.  Why is economic growth considered to be desirable?

3.  What are the main sources of economic growth?

4.  What are the disadvantages of rapid growth?

5.  How have governments attempted to improve growth rates?

163

# INDEX

# ADDITIONAL READING

Donaldson, P., 10 x Economics (Penguin 1982).

Harvey, J., Modern Economics, 4th Edition (Macmillan, 1983).

Kermally, S., Multiple Choice Economics, 1st Edition (Checkmate/Arnold, 1985).

Keynes, J.M., The General Theory of Employment, Interest and Money (Macmillan, 1981).

Lancaster, K., Modern Economics, Principles and Policy, 2nd Edition (Rand McNally, 1979).

Levick, J., Essential Topics for Examinations in Economics, 1st Edition (Checkmate/Arnold, 1985).

Lipsey, R.G., An Introduction to Positive Economics, 6th Edition (Weidenfeld & Nicolson, 1983).

Livesey, F., A Textbook of Economics, (Polytech Publishers, 1978).

Prest, A.R. & Coppock, D.J., The UK Economy: A Manual of Applied Economics, 9th Edition (Weidenfeld & Nicolson, 1982).

Samuelson, P.S., Economics, 11th Edition (McGraw-Hill, 1980).

Stanlake, G.F., Introductory Economics, 3rd Edition (Longman 1981).

Whitehead, G., Economics Made Simple (Heinemann, 1982).

Students should also attempt to keep abreast of developments by reading current periodicals such as The Economist, Bank Reviews and the Economic Progress Report published by the Treasury (available from the Publication Division, Central Office of Information, Hercules Road, London, SE1 7DU).

Useful sources of statistics are:—
    Economic Trends
    Annual Abstract of Statistics
    National Income and Expenditure
These publications are available in most libraries and give a comprehensive coverage of relevant statistics.

## THE BASIC CONCEPTS SERIES

The Basic Concepts series attempts to explain in a clear and concise manner the main concepts involved in a subject. Paragraphs are numbered for ease of reference and key points are emboldened for clear identification, with self assessment questions at the end of each chapter. The texts should prove useful to students studying for A level, professional and first year degree courses. Other titles in the series include:—

## QUESTIONS AND ANSWERS SERIES

These highly successful revision aids contain questions and answers based on actual examination questions and provide fully worked answers for each question. The books are written by experienced lecturers and examiners and will be useful for students preparing for O and A level, foundation and BTEC examinations. Subjects include:—

Economics by G. Walker
Accounting by T. Hines
Multiple Choice Economics by Dr. S. Kermally
O level Mathematics by R.H. Evans
A level Pure Mathematics and Statistics by R.H. Evans
A level Pure and Applied Mathematics by R.H. Evans
O level Physics by R.H. Evans
O level Chemistry by J. Sheen
O level Human Biology by D. Reese